Marc Ellis

Marc *Ellis*

crossing the line

with Kirsten Matthew

Hodder Moa

National Library of New Zealand Cataloguing-in-Publication Data
Ellis, Marc, 1971-
Marc Ellis : crossing the line / Marc Ellis with Kirsten Matthew.
ISBN-13: 978-1-86971-074-3
ISBN-10: 1-86971-074-6
1. Ellis, Marc, 1971- 2. Rugby football players—New
Zealand—Biography. I. Matthew, Kirsten. ll.Title.
796.333092—dc 22

Designed and produced by Hachette Livre NZ Ltd
Printed by Tien Wah Press Ltd, Singapore

Jacket photos: Juan Mon

To all the good buggers I've met

Contents

Preface

Writing this book has been a challenge, mostly because I have no idea whether anyone will care one iota for anything I have to say. Time has been a scarce resource in my life thus far and I haven't been able to contemplate taking a few months off to do something like this until now. To be honest, I haven't really felt like I've had too much to say in the past.

I'm pretty reserved when it comes to my private life, and I try to avoid publicity about my family and friends, but I do concede that I have a few stories to tell, and now's a good time to tell them. I'm moving on to a new chapter — I'm newly married and out of the day-to-day running of my business, Charlie's, and I have the time to sit down and give my side of a few stories, and to reflect on the journey.

I've been fortunate with the people I've met and I've had some lucky times. I've been in the right place at the right time for opportunities to happen, and when they have I've happily given my all.

I've been very lucky with the parents I was born to and the loving environment I grew up in; I had a charmed childhood. I'm lucky in the friends I've made. To cut a long story short, I've enjoyed a dream ride for the last 30-odd years.

I have also been fortunate that my desire to write this book coincided with my good friend Kirsten Matthew having time to do it with me. We have been friends for 20 years, and getting her home from New York (where she lives) and hanging out with her during the writing process has been a great bonus.

It has been interesting to sit down and document the significant events in my life up to now. I've never kept a diary, and my memory for certain things has faded, but fortunately some stories are permanently etched into my memory. Some bloody odd things have happened to me, that's for sure. And I hope this book succeeds in conveying them.

I've crammed a lot into life, probably because I'm driven by the need to have a crack and keep a smile. I won't die wondering. That likely explains some of my good and bad behaviour over the years, and why I've crossed the line a few times in my life. But always my intention has been to have fun.

This book is not a heavy read. It is made up of some of the more amusing things that I have been a part of, and how those experiences have shaped me. Some of them are a bit risqué and could be taken in the wrong way, but I hope not.

When I went off to varsity in Dunedin in 1991, my father gave me a cool piece of writing, 'Desiderata' by Max Ehrmann. It offers a blueprint of what's really important in life. It sat on my desk through university and has been something I have reflected on often over the years, in good and not-so-good times. I think you can do a lot worse than live your life by it.

Desiderata

Go placidly amid the noise and haste,
and remember what peace there may be in silence.
As far as possible without surrender
be on good terms with all persons.
Speak your truth quietly and clearly;
and listen to others,
even the dull and the ignorant;
they too have their story.

Avoid loud and aggressive persons,
they are vexations to the spirit.
If you compare yourself with others,
you may become vain and bitter;
for always there will be greater and lesser persons than yourself.
Enjoy your achievements as well as your plans.

Keep interested in your own career, however humble;
it is a real possession in the changing fortunes of time.
Exercise caution in your business affairs;
for the world is full of trickery.
But let this not blind you to what virtue there is;
many persons strive for high ideals;
and everywhere life is full of heroism.

Be yourself.
Especially, do not feign affection.
Neither be cynical about love;
for in the face of all aridity and disenchantment
it is as perennial as the grass.

Take kindly the counsel of the years,
gracefully surrendering the things of youth.
Nurture strength of spirit to shield you in sudden misfortune.
But do not distress yourself with dark imaginings.

Many fears are born of fatigue and loneliness.
Beyond a wholesome discipline,
be gentle with yourself.

You are a child of the universe,
no less than the trees and the stars;
you have a right to be here.
And whether or not it is clear to you,
no doubt the universe is unfolding as it should.

Therefore be at peace with God,
whatever you conceive Him to be,
and whatever your labours and aspirations,
in the noisy confusion of life keep peace with your soul.

With all its sham, drudgery, and broken dreams,
it is still a beautiful world.
Be cheerful.
Strive to be happy.

— Max Ehrmann, 1952

A Bit of a Show-off

I must have been about three when I started going across to the park with my dad on Saturday and Sunday mornings. I can remember so clearly the thrill I'd get on those mornings. The weekends were really something to look forward to.

Mum loved her sleep-ins, so we'd tiptoe around the house. Weekends would start with the kids' request show on the radio, which I would listen to in bed with Dad, then we'd head off to the park that was just up the road from our house in Wadestown, Wellington. Depending on the season we'd kick a rugby ball around or play a bit of cricket. We'd be there for four or five hours, until lunchtime.

Even at that age I'd have a go at tackling Dad. He'd run past me and because I was so small I'd usually grab onto only one leg. I'd have him by the ankle. He'd drag me along until I could loop my arms around the other leg too and eventually I'd bring him down. I'd never let go. Dad would be dragging me around the field, laughing, and I'd just cling on.

When we'd finished I was allowed a drink from the dairy — that was a real treat. It was always a toss-up between a can of fizz (Sparkling Duet) and a pint of ice-cold milk. We'd walk back down the hill and home to Mum, covered in grass stains and mud and ready for the garden hose.

* * *

I had a really happy childhood. I was born on 8 October 1971 and my parents, Chris and Anne, christened me Mark, after the All Black Mark Irwin. My middle names are Christopher Gwynne, so my initials are MCG, like the Melbourne Cricket Ground. My old man was a mad-keen cricketer, so it makes sense really.

Both my parents were into sports. Mum was a pretty good netballer and a championship diver in her day. Dad had one or two cricket games for Auckland in his heyday and almost played a game of rugby for the Auckland Maori side. He likes the sun, so he had a fairly good tan on when he was picked for the team, but he realised that his tan only covered so much and that he would be 'exposed' as an impostor in the changing room, and withdrew. By the time I came along Mum and Dad had moved to Wellington and Dad was playing senior cricket for Kilbirnie. Bruce Edgar was in that team. He was one of my heroes when I was young and I can still remember the day the whole team came to help Mum and Dad with extensions to the house. I was running around getting the drinks.

I'm an only child. Mum has always said she wouldn't have been able to cope with any more kids like me. I used to think I'd like to have an older brother and a sister (who would have been vitally important by the time I was 13 or 14 and interested in girls). It would have been quite cool to have somebody to share stuff with. On the other hand, I'm told you don't know what hate is until you have a sibling, and ignorance is bliss — I couldn't imagine what it was like to have brothers and sisters, so I was quite happy on my own. I had my cat, Rupert; he was as close as I came to a brother and he's probably why I've got a real soft spot for animals to this day.

Anne Ellis: He got all our attention. I don't think either of us could really have handled more than Marc, so it's fortunate we had only one child. But right from very early on we stressed the importance of sharing.

Chris Ellis: Marc was never spoilt. Certainly he wasn't disadvantaged in any way, but we were very conscious of the 'Only Child' syndrome. We went to Fiji quite a bit as a young family. When he was old enough, 12 or so, I said, 'Right, next year we will be going again and you are going to spend your own money rather than our money.' So he started a paper round. We made a trolley for him to carry the papers and on a Thursday night we would drag this trolley around the suburb. It was completely underpaid, but he learnt the value of money, the idea of getting paid to work, and he ended up with $50. In Fiji that year his mother paid for all his ice creams and so on, so I told him to spend his money at the duty free, before we left. He bought himself a cricket bat and a two-way walkie-talkie. On the flight home, I said, 'How does that feel, son? Isn't it better to spend your own money rather than somebody else's?' He said, 'No.' Little bugger — he just wasn't going to let me know that it was.

I don't remember much of my first five years, but I remember my first playgroup. It didn't turn out to be much fun and I didn't get to play much. The horrible woman who ran it would put us in the cupboard and pull us by the hair if we misbehaved. I complained to Mum and Dad, and they finally caught the 'wicked witch' in the act and I got rescued.

At the local kindergarten I got told off for doing my potato stamps on the walls and the floor instead of on my bit of paper. But I got in the good books when I spotted a fire at the house next door and was the first to raise the alarm.

I was a fairly energetic and mobile chap.

Chris Ellis: He was like one of those firecrackers you hold — a sparkler — he was full of electricity.

Anne Ellis: When he started school he had so much energy that they had to put the mats out in the hallway and give him gymnastics before class. He would tumble along the hallway and get out enough energy to be ready to sit down in class. Then, at night, after going all day, he'd stop. We had a rule in the house: one hour of television, three nights a week. I quickly learned that rather than tell him he'd seen his television for the week, it was far better to say, 'Sure, you have your bath, get yourself all ready and we will have dinner and then you can sit down and watch TV.' He would sit down to watch TV and within five minutes he would be dead to the world, out like a light. He just couldn't stay up. During the day he had all that energy, but then he'd crash.

I hadn't been at Wadestown Side School long before I was punished for showing off. Not really understanding girls and not being quite sure how to behave around them, I decided to throw an enormous amount of sand from the nearby sandpit at a group of them. It wasn't a great start.

Anne Ellis: I did Mothers' patrol on the pedestrian crossing one afternoon. Once all the children from the Side School had poured down the road and across the main street and everything was taken care of, I thought, 'Where the devil's Marc?' So I walked up the hill to the school, where I saw Sally Barrett, the headmistress. I said, 'You haven't seen Marc, have you?' She said, 'Yes, he's cleaning the Wendy House.' I looked up and there was this Wendy House. It was literally going 'huff, huff' — puffs of sand were coming out the doors and windows. It looked like a cartoon, the dust was flying everywhere. It was so funny. The little devil had bombarded the Wendy House with sand from the sandpit, so he was kept in after school and made to clean it. He never did it again.

But I did give others a bit of a hard time, as my teacher explained in my school report when I was six: 'Marc is still having problems in the classroom and has begun to tease other children in the playground. He can be one of the most sensitive members of the class, though, and I am hopeful that this side of his nature will blossom, especially when he enters the main school.'

The ride-on train set was the best toy in the New Entrants classroom and there was always a race for it at lunchtime. If you got the engine or the caboose, you were pretty cool; if you got one of the carriages in between you were a lemon. I figured out that I had to sit close to the door and be quick out of the blocks when the bell rang if I wanted the best bit. That's my first memory of really wanting to win something, I think. I didn't always hold on to the caboose; sometimes I got there, grabbed it, and then got beaten up by a bigger person who took it off me, but at least I'd got there first.

I was born competitive. It's in my genes — both Mum and Dad are competitive — and I think genetics give you a map that you don't stray far from. Competition motivated me in everything from a young age, and still does. I'm a big fan of competition, of kids having the chance to win. If you're not under pressure, if you're not competing with somebody else or with yourself, you're kind of wasting your time, I think. You are more likely to fall short of your potential. Nowadays children are rewarded for participation rather than winning. Every kid that goes in a race or enters a spelling bee is rewarded. The winner gets the same reward as the loser. That's just so wrong I reckon — kids *must* compete. All over the world competition helps sustain society on an individual, corporate and national level.

I've never met a kid who is a complete dud at everything. They all have a gift, whether it's an academic gift, a musical talent, a sporting ability. If they're the best in the class at something, we should let them know, let them feel good about that gift, and really have a crack at it. People need to know when they're good at things, and be congratulated when they are, and told to try harder when they're not so good at something. I wasn't ever good at maths, but if I moved up in the class I took a huge amount of pride in that — and made sure those I passed knew all about it, in the nicest possible way, of course. I was never going to get to number one, but every now and then I moved up because I was intent on competing, and for me that's been a positive thing.

My first crush was on a girl in New Entrants. Her name was Natasha Groves and she was bigger than me. I held her hand once on a school outing and knew straight away that life didn't get much better than that. I loved her. Sadly she didn't love me, despite my obvious endeavours to catch her attention. In fact, she didn't care for me at all.

One day Natasha walked past my house with her older sister. My friend Mark Lonergan and I were in the garage with Dad's boxing gloves on, having a play fight. Natasha's sister, who was about seven, came out of her way, into the garage, and said, 'Boxing's stupid'. I didn't know how to handle the humiliation, so I thumped her on the nose! I knew I wasn't ever allowed to hit girls, but I was so embarrassed I lashed out (and she *was* bigger than me). She ran home bawling and I got in real trouble when Dad found out what I had done. I decided I didn't really like girls after that and that didn't change for a long time.

By the time I was seven I had two great mates in the neighbourhood. Russell Penlington and Adam Brockey both lived a few doors down from me and we spent our weekends tearing around the block, building tree huts and trolleys and causing as much trouble as we could. Well, not really trouble — we were never milk bottle-money stealers and we never nicked anything from the local dairy — but we did fire the odd pea-shooter at cars and people on bikes.

I often got into trouble for high-spirited mischief — much as I do to this day — but never was my trouble-making malicious. Nor was it ever really bad. I was just cheeky. I get that from my old man; he's a bit of a show-off like me. At Guy Fawkes, especially, he was in his element. One year he claimed he was going to shoot a rocket across the gully into a neighbour's garden. He lined it up and shot that rocket right in their front window. Straight in. Then it started banging and fizzing. It was chaos — the people were jumping around their living room trying to put the rocket out. Dad hit the lights and raced around blowing out the candles in our garden and our Guy Fawkes ended abruptly with Mum, Dad and me hiding in the dark. It was a one-in-a-million shot and hardly grown-up adult Guy Fawkes conduct, but I loved it. After that I thought I was living with Superman himself. To this day I can't believe what a good shot he was.

I think that story helps explain my generally irresponsible behaviour; particularly as many years later, while at university, my friend Chiz and I were involved in another unsavoury Guy Fawkes episode. We went around to our friends' flat and started firing rockets into the house to freak out the five girls who lived there. Sadly, only one of the girls was home and, frightened, she holed up under the bed and called the police. When a car came up the driveway we loaded the crutches we were using as a rocket launcher and fired. Moments later we were being told to drop our weapons by the police!

Underneath it all I was a fairly respectful sort of kid actually. And I learnt very quickly that the best way to get out of trouble was to be really apologetic.

Chris Ellis: He always accepted discipline well. Anne and I knew what we thought was reasonable behaviour. He was a pretty active kid and he got a fair amount of correcting, but we'd explain the reasons why we were doing what we were doing, and he never got excessively angry about it. He was very reasonable about it.

There were lots of cool places to make forts in Wadestown, and in 1978 we had heaps of galas and fairs at school. That was a great year and if I could go back and relive a year in my childhood, I think it would be the year I was seven. The only bugger was that there were three of us mates mucking around, and three was a crowd sometimes; invariably two would gang up on the other and someone would go home crying. The odd one out was usually the tag-along, the one who didn't get up early enough to call around and arrange to play for the day, so I always tried to be the first to get on the phone. It was a balancing act between calling their households at a reasonable hour, not too early, but not so late that I missed out.

Usually I was allowed to take a mate along on our family holidays at Te Horo, an hour north of Wellington. They were fantastic holidays. My cousins would come and we'd all stay on a farm there. We were all about the same age and it was great fun for us city kids. We milked the cows, and then drank the warm milk out of the vats. We fed the pigs and the chickens. We played 'Go home, Stay home' most nights, in the bush that we called the Haunted Forest.

There was a haystack in the barn where we were told the possums lived. Dad would offer $5 (which felt like $1000 to us) to the kid who could sleep out in the hay barn all night. We couldn't set up our camp during the day — we had to leave for the barn once it got dark — and we had to stick it out for the whole night. It always sounded like a good idea, so we'd all traipse off at bedtime with our pillows and our sleeping bags. The parents would sit back and wait. Without fail we would settle in, then hear the hiss of a possum and be off like lightning through the fields back to the house, a trail of bedding left in our wakes. On my first attempt –- I must have been about eight — I walked straight into an electric fence and sprinted home howling. I didn't even reach the barn.

Up the road from the farm lived a guy everyone called Nudie Man. The Nudie Man lived on a corner section and had made a garden out of metal flowers and pieces of rubbish. His house was an absolute shambles, like something out of 'Hansel and Gretel', and he spent every day in his tin garden wearing just a loincloth. He fascinated us.

We used to ride past on our bikes and yell out to him, 'Nudie Man, Nudie Man', then crack up laughing. He didn't find it that funny, but it was a lot of fun, and probably my first taste of the joys of nudity.

I spent a lot of time with my grandfather too. We used to do heaps of cool stuff; go whitebaiting at Waikanae, and hang out together. He was a good dude.

Anne Ellis: My father and Marc had a very similar sense of humour; they were just delightful to see together. They were very close.

When he died, it was my first experience of losing somebody that I loved. I vividly remember hearing the phone ring really early on a Saturday morning. My father came into my bedroom and told me that Mum's dad had died, and that I was going to have to be strong. I decided that I would change the spelling of my name to Marc because Granddad always thought that Mark with a 'k' was a bit harsh.

Since then I've had all of my grandparents pass on. Each one meant a lot to me, but my maternal grandfather was particularly special.

* * *

I think I was probably born with a natural ability to catch a ball and run with it, but I definitely had more of a challenge in the classroom. I was easily distracted and prone to playing the goat. When I was eight I came home with this on my school report: 'Marc has been applying himself to his work with more enthusiasm as the year has progressed. He is easily distracted by others in the class, but lately has been voluntarily going to a desk on his own where he can work quietly without distractions. He is inclined to act before he thinks of the consequences. Marc enjoys physical activities and should be capable at sports such as soccer as he gets older.'

Parent-teacher meetings could be dicey too, and after one particular meeting at the school my parents decided Wadestown Side School wasn't the best place for me. Apparently, the headmaster stood up and said, 'Don't worry; it is not unusual for children to leave this school with a reading age of eight. It's more important that they are happy and well adjusted.'

It was the late 70s: women had hairy armpits and teachers were anti-competition, but my parents didn't buy into that philosophy. They were absolutely appalled and they decided that it was time for me to go to a school that had the same philosophy as them. So they sent me to Wellesley College.

Chris Ellis: We reluctantly pulled him out of a state school education. I'm a strong believer in a public school education, but Marc is fiercely competitive and target driven — he wanted to win maths, be the best at sport — and at Wadestown School the kids could come last and still get patted on the head, which was confusing to him. One of the most important things was that, unlike Wadestown School, Wellesley College was structured. The school set him boundaries and goals and targets. The standards and values set at school were in absolute harmony with the way that he was brought up at home and there was no conflict. He knew his boundaries.

Anne Ellis: That was the best decision we ever made because their philosophy was self-discipline. Marc of course had a go at everything — and it was a longer day, which suited him.

Wellesley College was such a great school. It was in Eastbourne so we had the beach right there and the bush behind it. It was such a splendid setting. It cost a bit to go to, but there were great upsides for me at a school like that. Even if I did get a hard time in the beginning.

Chris Ellis: One day, just after he started at Wellesley, Marc caught the bus to school. Some older boys on the bus started teasing him, telling him he was on the wrong bus. Eventually, they bullied him off the bus and he walked home in tears, which was understandable. I just happened to be late leaving for work, so I was home when he arrived. His mother was arranging to drive him to school, but I stopped her and made Marc catch the next bus. It was hard to do, but it would have been harder for him if he'd got a ride. He had to catch the bus that day and get it over with.

Some mornings I would catch the bus to Eastbourne with the workers from the Ford factory in Petone. I made friends with a big Island fella called Sonny, and our friendship gave me my first taste of economics. Well, sort of. Dad worked for Cyclax (a cosmetic company started in

New Zealand by his father) and I asked him for a bottle of perfume to give my teacher for her birthday. Then I swapped it with Sonny (who was going to take it home for his wife) for a homemade chocolate cake.

I loved sports, any sports at all — swimming, rugby, Aussie rules, cross country; you name it, I had a crack at it. I joined my first rugby club, Karori, when I was eight. There were about four guys in the team who used to score a lot of tries. We'd all get more than 100 points during the season. I did the goal-kicking and I was greedy with the ball in hand, which didn't ever change.

I'd always be so excited to get out and play cricket or rugby on a Saturday morning that if it were ever cancelled I'd cry. Wellington's weather being what it is — highly volatile and unpredictable — that happened about 50 per cent of the time and I'd always be devastated.

Often we played in atrocious conditions. It wasn't just the cold. It was the wind, which would lick along Western Park. We'd literally have to lean into it. Sometimes it was so cold that we'd run out onto ice — our feet going clomp, clomp. If I got tired and had a sit-down, the sheet ice would crack underneath me. One particular day it was so cold all the boys ran around crying — no one wanted to touch the ball or make tackles or do anything. The worst thing about the bad weather was the sight of the parents all rugged up and warm, standing on the sideline.

Chris Ellis: Without fail we'd go to watch, only because we enjoyed it, not because we felt that we had a duty to do it. He had our total support.

Dad always had an appalling dress sense and in the 70s he was sporting a heavy moustache and an Afro. In my teenage years he got into après-ski gear: he bought moon boots, a red all-in-one snowsuit with matching red gloves, and a red crocheted hat, and wore them when he came to watch me play rugby. Everyone else's parents were dressed in Swanndris and gumboots and my dad looked like he'd just skied off the slopes of Chamonix. He was like a beacon on the sideline; he was almost glowing. I would be trying to call moves from first-five and my best mate Simon, who played centre, would be winding me up, yelling, 'Forget about the move! Look at your old man!'.

On the weekends I loved to go to Athletic Park with Dad and watch the Wellington team play. We would get to Newtown on a Saturday afternoon, and all I wanted was a hot dog, and to see the guys run around the field.

My uncle, Mick Williment (who married Dad's sister), was an All Black and once I understood what that meant I really looked up to him. His rugby career was over by the time I came along, but he played fullback for Wellington and played for the All Blacks in the 60s. He had a prodigious kicking game and was a great guy, and as I grew up I started to appreciate his experience as an All Black.

In the late 70s and early 80s, the Wellington rugby team was a fantastic team. Murray Mexted was my hero and Bernie Fraser, Stu Wilson and Jock Hobbs were all beaut players too. After the games I'd run on with all the other kids and try to touch my favourite players on the back. I was too scared to talk to them, or ask for an autograph, which seems silly now that I know all those guys, that I've worked with some of them and had a beer or two with them, but that was how in awe of them I was back then. They were grown-ups who, as I saw it, did heroic deeds, and I desperately wanted to touch them.

Jock Hobbs, ex-All Black, chairman of the New Zealand Rugby Union: I first met Marc in 1983. I didn't know it was him at the time, though. It was while the Lions were on tour. I was part of the team that played against them and I was asked to go to Wellesley College to talk to the first XV. After the talk, as I was saying goodbye, a young boy came running up and tugged on my jacket, then ran back to the safety of his class. Later, when I got to know Marc in the New Zealand Universities side, he confessed it was him.

When I was 10 I got into the local Hutt Valley representative cricket side. Of all the games I've ever played in my life, cricket is my favourite. I love cricket. I love the mental aspect of the game, how you can psych people out. There's more to it than the physical aspect of it sometimes. You can be any shape and size and still play. While rugby is very much a team game, cricket is both a team game and a fantastic individual game. I still play cricket now and I just love spending a whole day in the sun with my mates, having a laugh.

The Hutt Valley side was a really cool team. Heath Davis was in it, as was Simon Mannix (who came to be one of my fierce rivals in rugby at first-five). At that time Richard Hadlee was the opening bowler for New Zealand and Heath, by the age of 12, could bowl as fast as Hadlee. He was our lethal weapon. Facing him on a concrete wicket was the most terrifying thing. Helmets hadn't been heard of in those days; if a ball landed in the wrong place you could be in serious trouble, so kids would just throw their bat at his ball and run off. At an Auckland tournament once (the first time to the Big Smoke for a lot of us) Heath came charging in with a bouncer and hit the Auckland opener on the head. He collapsed and fell on his wickets. We started yelling, 'You're out, you're out!' We didn't care that he was helped off. We were just pleased we'd got him out.

That same year I made the Wellesley College first XV as a hooker. Thankfully, that didn't continue for too long and the next year I was on the wing, which I loved. I daydreamed about playing on Athletic Park one day, like Murray Mexted and Jock Hobbs, and I was thrilled the day we got to play as part of a curtain-raiser to a curtain-raiser at Athletic Park. I was so excited, got so revved up, I maniacally whizzed around the field and ended up being named Player of the Day.

Chris Ellis: From a young age he excelled under pressure. He preferred it when there was some pressure on. A good example is that as a kid, about 12 years of age, he would consistently kick goals from the sideline. Even in wet weather he could do that, and that was difficult for an adult. But put him in an easier position, closer to the posts, and he'd sometimes miss. Not always but sometimes.

I was spending a lot of afternoons up at the park by myself by that time, practising my goal-kicking after school. There was a tree that I used as a goalpost and I'd happily kick the ball over it for hours on end. One afternoon, as I was kicking away, a car pulled up at the edge of the park. The window slowly rolled down. A head came out and this deep voice boomed, 'Good kick, lad'. It was Murray Mexted! I picked up the ball and sprinted home to tell Mum, and I don't think my feet touched the ground the whole way home.

Shenanigans

My dad's always been my greatest mate. If ever I've needed someone to talk to, he's been there. He was at every game of cricket I played, every game of rugby. He took time off work so he could come to my inter-school matches. When I made the All Blacks I'd ring him before every game. No matter what time of the day or night it was, where in the world I was calling from, he'd talk to me, say the things I wanted to hear, tell me not to be nervous, to go out and have some fun on the field. Mum's always been really supportive too, just as much as Dad. I'm really lucky I've got two of the most loyal, dedicated people in my corner.

My first day at Wellington College, I got a bit of a speech from my father. He told me I'd have to observe a bit, learn the ropes, and stand up to a few people. That first day at Wellington College I met my best mate Simon Neal. We were both at Wellington Railway Station, waiting for the train. We paired up and, as luck would have it, were in the same class. Simon was a lot smarter than me. He had the ability, if he'd done some work every now and then, to be in an A-stream class, but he didn't want to so we were lucky enough to stay in the same class right through high school. We made some great mates at school. We had a crew of 10 or so guys who are still some of my top mates.

We had a great deal of fun and often turned a boring class into a really fun one. We certainly got up to some shenanigans.

There was a hierarchy at Wellington College and you had to pick your allies. You couldn't sit down the back of the bus. The back seat was for the seniors, so if you were silly enough to try it, you got removed, often forcibly. (There was a similar hierarchy in the All Blacks years later.) You couldn't fight it and be a smart-arse, it was just the way it was. It was a game and it was a matter of understanding it and learning how to play along.

One of the first things I did was offer to carry a prefect's bag off the bus and up the drive. It was a strategy: pick some key guys who would come in handy and get them on-side. In those days there were only 12 prefects, so they were held in very high regard. If you got off-side with them, your number was definitely up.

The strategy worked. There were always fights at school, and when a guy a lot bigger than me picked a fight I kept my guard up and punched straight and I didn't do badly, until the guy turned. If he'd collared me I'd have been in trouble, but three of the prefects (whose bags I carried on a regular basis) were in the crowd watching. The moment he laid into me they pulled him off and broke it up, which was pretty lucky really.

If you kept your nose clean and went about your business, there were no problems at school. If you pushed it, you knew about it. One day at lunchtime I wound up Steve Guinea, the older brother of a boy I played rugby with. Steve was about as tough as they came at school. I took off, but he caught me and pulled a roll of duct tape out of his bag. As the bell that signalled the end of lunch rang, he taped my arms and legs together, and my whole head up, and left me on one of the paddocks. I couldn't see and had just one nostril free to breathe with. While I was pissed off at being caught I thought it was brilliant — I'd managed to get the attention of the first XV captain, a prefect who was pretty hard-case — and later, when I was a senior, I did similar things to the younger guys (who I knew had a sense of humour).

There were some wonderful teachers at Wellington College. A lot of them had great senses of humour, and knew how to get the best out of young guys. I liked 95 per cent of them, even if I didn't always appreciate them at the time.

If we deserved it, they gave us the odd welt. I don't agree with the bleeding hearts against corporal punishment. Teachers are too limited in the way they can deal with kids now, and corporal punishment really worked for me. I narrowly avoided ever getting caned by the headmaster, either because I was good at talking my way out of it, or at figuring out just when to pull back and stop playing up, but like a lot of my friends I became very familiar with 'Oscar', the leather strap one of the science teachers carried like a truncheon in his pocket. I copped Oscar over the knuckles on several occasions. In the end I volunteered to look after the rats' cages in the science lab, and Oscar paid me little attention thereafter.

We had a healthy respect for our teachers' authority, but we also pushed the boundaries a wee bit. A third-form teacher, Mr Oaks, had an interesting time of it; mind you, he used to throw dusters at boys. He once grabbed Simon for being cheeky and thumped his head into the blackboard (which I greatly enjoyed).

Our response to this was to wind him up further. While Mr Oaks was writing on the board we would quietly get everyone down the back of the class in a big huddle. When the time was right we would start chanting 'Scrap, scrap, scrap'. Mr Oaks would come charging down, screaming, 'Break it up, break it up', and we would all be pointing at a scrap of paper on the floor. He fell for it a few times.

A few years later Mr Oaks went off for a hip operation and came back as a relieving teacher. When we knew that we had him as our reliever we all sauntered into class five or 10 minutes late. As one boy straggled in after another Mr Oaks became more and more irate. When a guy called Rhys came in 20 minutes late, offering up some ridiculous excuse about someone having hidden his pencil case, it was the last straw. We all rolled our eyes and suggested to Mr Oaks that Rhys was mocking him to his face. Mr Oaks took a full swing with his cane at Rhys' hamstrings. The momentum of the swing saw his hip give way a little and poor old Mr Oaks sprawled on the floor, much to our collective amusement.

Another day he took us up to the top field for a game of rounders and when we got up there we ran off. By the time Mr Oaks got down the hill on his bad hip, we were all sitting on the bus ready to go home.

Mr Sowby was obsessed with hand grenades. If you got him started on them he could waste the best part of a class on how to throw one. We'd come to class with pinecones in our pockets and someone would say, 'Mr Sowby, if we're going to get invaded, we need to know how to use a grenade'. That always worked a treat. He'd show us how to bite the pin out and then throw the 'grenade' like a googly, saying, 'Out the back of the hand boys, out the back of the hand'.

One day, in the fourth form, one of the boys brought a *Penthouse* to class. Our teacher, who was a great bloke, was writing away on the board. When he turned around we were all crowded around this kid's desk having a look. 'Bring that up here immediately,' he said. The boy nervously walked up to the board. 'Quiet reading,' the teacher announced, and he put his feet up on the desk and perused the dirty mag from behind his newspaper for the rest of class. That one small act earned our respect immediately. Imagine the uproar if that occurred in today's PC school environment.

Mr Murphy, an English teacher, was also the first XV coach. He used to inspect our nails and check that we were wearing garters and had the right belt on. He was meticulous, a real stickler for detail — he always wore a beautifully pressed suit with a matching handkerchief and he drove a green Hillman Super Minx that was immaculate. He was the 1960s personified and I loved that. I'm a bit of a stickler too, so to have a teacher like him was great for me. I think he must have liked me too, because when he took the first XV to Canada, he billeted me with his former wife and daughter. His daughter was very cute and I was the envy of the team.

During our lunch breaks in the summer months Simon, our mate Andrew Wilson, and I would unwind a fire hose from one of the old prefab classrooms and put it among the toetoe on the edge of the nearby basketball court. We would wait patiently for someone to walk within firing distance and unload the fire hose in their face. By the time they realised what had happened we would be well gone. It nearly went pear-shaped one day when, bored with squirting students, we decided to up the stakes and hit a teacher. As we beat a hasty retreat we were collared by another teacher we called Toad. Toad took us for PE and was a really good dude, but we knew we'd pushed it this time. We walked over to him, heads hung low, awaiting our punishment. Toad was silent for a minute, then said, 'Good shot!' and gave us a wink.

Fifteen years later Toad called me up and asked me to do a charity swim called Four Harbours. We swam Dunedin, Lyttelton, Wellington and Auckland harbours in the same day and raised $300,000 for CanTeen. It was on a flight to Dunedin that day that I first laid eyes on my wife to be, Agustina.

Students weren't allowed to use the teachers' lift. Walking up the stairs was fairly average, especially if you were going to the fifth floor for a class, so we used to pull our jerseys over our heads, jump in the lift and hope for the best. At the top we'd peel back the doors just enough to see if there was a teacher waiting, and if there was we'd jam the door shut and try the next floor. Mr Haskell, our first XI coach and a former Wellington cricketer, was a bit of a character. He told us he'd seen UFOs in the Wadestown gully -— evidently he enjoyed a wine or two of an evening. He was the only teacher who, if he caught you in the lift, would make you drop and do 20 press-ups, then send you on your way.

The teachers' toilets were off-limits too. There was one on every floor and they each had a single toilet stall and a separate hand-basin. The kids' toilets were a catastrophe, with industrial wax paper, so when possible I snuck into the teachers' (which were clean and had three-ply toilet paper). A teacher came in once while I was in the stall. He must have been desperate because he didn't leave when he saw the toilet was occupied.

'Who's in there?' he called out after a while. 'Cormack', I replied. It was a foolish choice: Cormack was a rather rotund teacher with a very deep voice, a voice far deeper than mine, so the teacher knew he had an impostor on his hands and I knew I was in real trouble.

I couldn't jump out the window — I was on the fifth floor. I was wearing a black team jersey; if I pulled it over my head and ran out,

I'd identify myself as a member of one of the top teams, increasing the chance of capture. As luck had it, I had a normal grey school jersey in my bag, so I put that on, pulled it up over my face, and threw my backpack out the window (which nearly killed a third-former below, according to school legend). I burst out of the stall, gave the teacher a healthy shove, and bolted off down the corridor.

I was unlucky because the teacher happened to be Mr Durant, the soccer coach and a top runner, and a high-speed chase ensued. Looking through the weave of a school jersey while moving at pace is surprisingly difficult and we went up and down stairs and through corridors for ages, before I got away from him. I'm sure Mr Durant knew it was me, but he could never prove it. Whenever I saw him afterwards I'd give him a cheeky smile and comment on how fit he looked.

Chris Ellis: He wasn't the perfect model pupil. He got up to practical jokes and that sort of thing. He was a loveable larrikin. We escaped any major trauma with him, but occasionally we had to pull him into line.

The funniest thing that ever happened at school was during an Anzac Day assembly. There must have been about 1200 kids gathered in the hall. All the teachers and the headmaster were on the stage in their hats and gowns. Sir Paul Reeves, the Governor-General, was the special guest.

A boy from the school band walked onto the stage and took his place to play 'The Last Post' on his bugle. It was a big honour and he started off with aplomb, but shortly thereafter suffered every bugle-player's nightmare — an off note — and a murmur of amusement immediately rippled through the school hall. The poor bugger must have been very nervous about his ability to pull the whole thing off, because once he cocked up, the bad notes started to come thick and fast.

It was a real assault on the ears and knowing that the Governor-General was in attendance and that we had to keep it cool made it even funnier. Soon the whole hall was shuddering; even the teachers were giggling. Simon and I were sitting together and tears of laughter were pooling at our feet.

Eventually, the headmaster had to silence the music. He made a gruff speech about discipline and respect, then gave the nod to the bugler to finish the solo. We waited with bated breath. The now-terrified musician stepped forward and started with a loud honk and the school erupted with hysterics. It was perfect.

Rumour has it the bugler left school shortly after that. I always thought he was a hero and if I could relive any moment of my life I would probably choose that.

There were a few staff members who didn't like me. One, Miss MacLean, had her favourites and I wasn't one of them. She was a large lady. In study class one day Simon and I drew a scale map of the library, where she worked as head librarian. Our plan was to sneak in on a Friday night in balaclavas, padlock her to her desk, padlock shut the doors, and leave her for the weekend. When another teacher caught us reviewing the plan he had a bit of a chuckle and apologetically said, 'I'm going to have to rip this up boys'.

I was never going to be an academic, and I went through school being told I should get School Certificate, might even get University Entrance, but I'd never get a degree (I was happy to prove everyone wrong on that one). I probably wasn't the most diligent student in the world, but there was an expectation that I had to work, certainly from my parents, and I did do my schoolwork. In my School C year I got a tutor for maths and that ended up being one of my better subjects, and I passed every subject.

Chris Ellis: Marc has the ability to sit down and be attentive, if it takes his fancy. But if there is no, as he perceives it, pressure, he's quite a different person. With his bountiful energy, he used to be like a top and difficult sometimes to nail down. He'd come through the door, drop his bag and shoot off. Sometimes it was impossible to know if our instructions or commands had been taken on board. We made sure he understood what was going on and that we understood that he understood by saying to him, 'Stop, listen, do it'. Those three commands worked: 'Stop', because he wouldn't stop unless you told him too. 'Listen', to make sure he heard what we were saying, and 'Do it', so we knew it would get done.

I got UE in seventh form, but missed a B Bursary by a few marks, so I went back to school and did another year in the seventh form. Simon came with me. He'd done much better than me in the exams, so why he came back I don't know, but I'm glad he did.

I think there's something about me and institutions and hanging on because it wasn't only Wellington College where I took longer than most — I managed to stay five years at university. It's the same at a party; I don't mind hanging in there if it's a good time.

* * *

Wellington College was known for its sporting abilities. We were able to participate at the top of all the secondary school divisions in most sports. I was in the A teams for rugby and cricket that year, and I couldn't wait till I made the first XV and the first XI.

At the end of the third form I was diagnosed with osteochondritis in my knees. It's a condition where not enough blood gets to the bone and pieces of bone or cartilage break away. It was causing horrible pains in my knees after sport and they would blow up and swell like sausages. It was an unlucky thing to get and a prick of a thing to have in the knees and my parents sought the advice of a Wellington specialist who decided to immobilise me. I had a cast on one leg from ankle to hip for six months. The cast was on morning, noon and night. That was the end of cricket, rugby, any sports at all, for half of the fourth form.

I became the manager of the rugby team I would have been in, just so I could be involved. I would turn up on my peg leg with the bottles of water and the halftime oranges. I enjoyed it as it kept me in the game and I liked organising, but it was incredibly frustrating to be stuck on the sideline watching and waiting.

When the cast came off the osteochondritis hadn't gone. I was itching to get back to sports of any kind so I decided to just rip into things and hope for the best. My leg was completely withered and I had to relearn to walk and run.

Not long after, we had the school sports. As usual I entered everything, and couldn't believe it when I won all the sprints. I was faster than I'd ever been. It was like I had gained a whole other gear. I guess the sheer frustration of being immobile for so long had its benefits.

My folks prior to my arrival.

Mum and Dad on the beach in Malaysia. I inherited my father's skinny legs.

Hanging out with my granddad and cousin Nicky.

The grumpy look . . .

First touch of the 'pigskin'.

The Ellis clan, 1975. Mum ran with the Princess Leia look back then.

Farm animals freaked me out at the age of two.

I was always stoked at the annual Christmas Parade.

Feeding my cat Rupert a lump of butter.

First day of school.

A page dedicated entirely to my father's dress sense — he had a special appreciation of fashion.

'Cheerios' — every kid's party favourite. My late uncle Mick Williment, an All Black in the 1960s, is in the background.

Me and my mate Russell on his pink ride.

Playing for Wellesley College with my best friend Mark Lonergan.

The 'Basin' ice-cream cart, on which I first worked with Stefan, aged 11.

Left: Taupo, 1988. Summer holidays were what we lived for at school. Shortly after this shot was taken we had to pull tents and leave. My mate's parents had rented the bach to some foreigners who didn't like us camped in the garden.

Below: Me (black singlet) running second in a Wellington senior schools 200-metre event. I was a year — and a few yards — behind these guys.

The boys posing with some free beer I'd scored from my summer job at O'Reilly's bottle store. The beer was three years past its use-by date and, as we discovered, completely undrinkable.

My first love, and still a great friend, Tiff Brown.

Chris Ellis: When he was about 11 or 12 he was quite awkward. He had a good eye for the ball but he had no natural speed, no real anything that made him stand out. It wasn't until he had his leg in traction due to the osteochondritis that he changed. That cast came off and he was a tearaway. His rugby took on a new dimension: he had the hand-ball combination, and now he had the speed. He wasn't physically mature, but he had ability, there were certain things he could do.

I managed to get into the second XI for a couple of cricket games at the end of that year. I had desperately wanted to be in the first XI, which Simon had got into, but didn't. In the fifth form I hoped to make the first XV, but I was put in 2A, the premier division for smaller boys.

The following year, 1988, I made it into the first XV and the first XI. I became captain of the cricket team, which meant I got my name in the pavilion, and I took it very seriously. I was just so keen to be there, in teams that I had wanted to be in since I started school.

I made the Central Regions rugby team too. I was marking guys who were 19 years old and a lot bigger than me. That didn't worry me, I knew how to duck and sidestep. I couldn't afford to tackle high — the big guys would throw me off — so I'd go for the legs, around the ankles.

Chris Ellis: People started to say to me, at school matches and rep games, 'He could be an All Black'. I'd say, 'Oh, yeah'. I didn't believe it, and it made me uncomfortable to hear that, so I had to divorce myself from those conversations — I'd go and stand under the goalposts rather than on the sideline. Then one day I gave one of his teachers a ride home. He was somebody who had the potential to make a call on something like that, and he said Marc was good enough to be an All Black. He actually eyeballed me as he said it and I had to change the way I thought. I didn't act any differently though. School still had to be his priority.

We had some bloody good rugby players at school. We had Perry Freshwater, who plays in England now, and Filo Tiatia, who played for Wellington and the All Blacks. The three of us got into the New Zealand Secondary Schools team in 1988. In a team like that you meet people from all walks of life. The cool thing you learn from that is how to mix with all sorts of people. In rugby you tend to gravitate to the people who are fairly close to your position on the field. The backs tend to be pretty chilled out and casual, whereas the forwards are a bit more intense. There were always a few guys in those rep teams that I'd get on really well with. We'd become thick as thieves and cause a bit of trouble.

There were guys I played rugby with who were really, really good, better than me, but never got very far. Maybe they got injured. Or maybe they didn't want it as much as guys like me, because I think in sport, and life, that is the key. If you want it badly enough and have the talent, you'll get there. That's where a competitive nature helps. You can't want it without being competitive.

In seventh form I made the Wellington Under-18 cricket team, the Secondary Schools rugby side, and the Colts, the Under-19 national rugby team. I knew that team wasn't too many steps away from the All Blacks and when I went to watch Wellington play at Athletic Park I started to think about how I'd play if I were on the field. I knew I was probably as fast as Lolani Koko or Mike Clamp, and for the first time I started to think I might be able to do the job they were doing.

That year I got a Mizuno sponsorship deal from Jock Hobbs (who had brought the Mizuno franchise into New Zealand).

Jock Hobbs: I recall coaching a side that played against the first XV at Wellington College. Marc played in that game and played outstandingly well. I could tell he was marked for greater things. He had a very high level of skills.

I signed a contract for my last year of school and first two years at varsity. I think it was worth $5000 a year, which was a lot of money.

Our arch-enemies at school were the St Pat's boys, the 'Dooleys'. Two of my mates at school were rough buggers who used to drive in to school from Wainui in a Datsun 120Y ute. On the way home from school they would go past a couple of local bakeries and pick up the day-old custard squares and doughnuts to feed to their pigs. We used to jump in the back of the ute and go with them. If they looked alright and came out of a clean-ish bin, we'd feast on the custard squares. If they were a bit rough we drove past the St Pat's school bus and threw them at anyone we recognised.

In my last couple of years at school I went to the McEvedy Shield, the yearly athletics competition between Wellington College, the two St Pat's schools, and Rongotai College. McEvedy included every track and field event you could imagine, and was the pinnacle of the rivalry between the Catholics and the Anglicans. Rongotai College was pretty hard to beat: they had a strong Pacific Island contingent of natural athletes. But we loved to beat the Dooleys. The prefects were in charge of coming up with school chants to put the other teams off at McEvedy. We had official chants we'd sing when the teachers were in earshot, and unofficial ones directed at the Dooleys that we'd launch into as soon as the teachers left.

Any rugby game between our first XV and St Pat's was hotly contested, especially if it was a home game. They were the games the season was judged on.

Earle Kirton, ex-All Black, All Blacks selector and assistant coach: I got tied up at St Pat's Silverstream helping out with rugby. Wellington had a very good first XV. The coach, Father Blake, said, 'We got a drubbing last week from Wellington College. They've got a very good player, Marc Ellis.' I went and watched him play against Upper Hutt and thought, 'By Jove, you're a talented bugger'. He had tremendous natural ability. If Silverstream was going to win, I had to start negating his ability. I changed the St Pat's first XV around, put a mad blindside flanker in at number seven. Then I said to myself, 'Shit, for the first time I've modified a game plan for one guy'. After that game I rang Marc up and asked him if he'd play in the Wellington Sevens. There had never been a schoolboy in a national squad like that. But it didn't eventuate because he went to Otago.

I got dropped as captain of the first XI in my second year in the seventh form. We went away for a pre-season warm-up game and got beaten. We all took it as a bit of a joke and perhaps I'd stopped taking my position so seriously, and my speech after the game reflected that (it was hard to take a match seriously when we were playing on astroturf). But it was also an opportunity for one of the teachers to push her son (who was a great cricketer) into the role of captain. As it happened he only lasted a few games before he had to stand down as captain too, after getting caught in a Napier pub at the end of a two-day game against Napier Boys'. We had got away with the same thing the year before, but only just: I was to make the speech on behalf of the schools' 15-odd summer teams, but when I came back late (chewing plenty of gum to hide the beer breath) the speech had been delivered by someone else. It was probably just as well, as I had a fair glow on by then.

After I was dropped as captain Simon and I told them to stick it and went to play club cricket, but the grade was not a challenge and eventually we both gave it up altogether, including the Under-18 rep team we were in. That was a really difficult decision to make, but by then rugby was taking up a lot of time.

My social life had also become pretty important and I'd well and truly rediscovered an interest in girls. My first date had been when I was 12, with a girl from Chilton Saint James School. I wore white sneakers, white Canterbury zip pants, and a red fishnet Chinese collared T-shirt (the 80s were foul times for fashion). We went to McDonald's, then to the movies. My mother played chaperone. I didn't get to kiss my date, which was a big disappointment, and I had to wait another year for my first kiss. It was at a Blue Light Rage, run by the police, in the Wellington Town Hall. It was always quite hard work to make an impression on the ladies at a Blue Light Rage, as there were much older guys, 16- and 17-year-olds, there. But I did pretty well this particular night and had my first kiss as I was dancing to 'Come on Eileen' (the 80s were also foul musically).

When I was 16 I started going out with my first serious girlfriend, Tiffany Brown. She was a Queen Margaret College girl. There was huge rivalry between Wellington College and the other boys' schools to see who could get on-side with the Queen Margaret girls. The Marsden College girls didn't quite cut it, there were a few nice girls at Wellington Girls', but the Queen Margaret girls epitomised all you could want in a girlfriend. They looked hot in their school smocks and they all loved a night out, plus most of them had beach houses and ski chalets.

Tiff was such a cool, laidback person. We had a great time together and stayed together until I went away to university. On a Thursday night we used to meet at a pub called the Southern Cross. The Southern was the watering hole for every kid under 20 in Wellington. Jugs of beer were $2 on a Thursday. I'd leave rugby practice with my mates, we'd change into jeans and T-shirts, arrive at the pub, and give our school bags stuffed with our uniforms and school books to the lady behind the counter. With $10 I could afford four jugs *and* a bite on the way home and in those days I never got anything like a hangover. I think Mum and Dad knew I was going for one or two after practice, but they were never quite sure just how many one or two entailed.

Every now and then one or other of our mates would have a party at home, usually while their parents were away. A group of bogans known as the Karori Boys were always bit of a problem. They got wind of every single party and turned up uninvited and unwelcome. As with most bogans they came by the tribe, in their Toranas and Cortinas, with their mullets flapping over their leather jackets. They'd usually drink the booze, put on their favourite George Thorogood tape, flog the coin jar in the parents' room, and have a crack at your girlfriend. If you got on the wrong side of them you got a hell of a hiding so we'd let them get away with it, but a few of them found the odd vengeful gift in their cars and jackets.

One evening after the pub my mate foolishly decided to drive his mother's car home even though we were a bit shickered. He suggested we put our school uniforms back on, just in case we got pulled over by the police. It was a brilliant idea because that's exactly what happened; a cop pulled us over and informed us that we didn't have our lights on. 'We've just been at a study group', my mate explained, 'and we got a flat battery, so we're driving home with our lights off'. The policeman suggested we stick to the main roads, as they had better street lighting, and told us to drive home safely.

When I was 18 I was caught drink driving and I went home beside myself. My old man used to berate me about the small things. 'If Dad grills me over the small things', I thought, 'what's he going to do over something this big?'. Instead, he came down to my room, gave me a kiss, and told me to get some sleep. It was the total opposite to what

I'd anticipated. My parents spent their lives getting the small things right, in the hope that the big things wouldn't happen, but when they did happen they were just as supportive as ever.

On a Friday night, after Mum and Dad had gone to bed, I used to climb out my bedroom window, shimmy down the drainpipe, and run from Wadestown to Tiff's place in Khandallah (about 10 kilometres). I'd run back before 5.30 a.m., when my old man woke up. It didn't matter that I'd had no sleep: I'd have a fry-up for breakfast and run off to rugby for the day.

In my last year at Wellington College, my second year in the seventh form, I became a prefect. By then the number of prefects had gone from 12 to more than 50, so it was no longer a position of respect.

I was put in charge of the last thing I should ever have been put in charge of, discipline, and my first day as prefect I staked out the tuck shop. The school rule was that boys weren't allowed to eat inside the tuck shop; they had to wait until they were outside. Anyone caught eating inside could get a prefect's detention. I wasn't too keen on giving those, because that meant staying after school supervising kids, but I was keen on some free food. So I nabbed a fifth-former as he took a chomp out of his lunch and said, 'Look, I don't want to do this, but you have two choices. You either give me your filled roll, or you get a detention.' I knew full well that he'd take the latter, so for his detention I made him carry a bucket full of sand up and down the rugby field. Then I made him carry the bucket above his head, up and down the terraces in front of the school while singing about being a sinner. The aim was to make a spectacle of the guy, so that no one ever wanted a detention from me, and it worked a treat. Everyone knew to avoid one of my prefect's detentions at all costs and the next guy I caught gladly handed over his filled roll. I ate for free every day. It was wonderful while it lasted, but too good to last — after a few months someone reported my scam to the headmaster and I was reprimanded.

Scarfieville

The day I moved into University College hostel I pulled back the curtains and looked out at Otago University and the surrounding streets. Directly below my room, on Clyde Street, my attention was drawn to a group of guys wearing overalls. I watched as they walked into a flat and came back out with a TV. They sat it on the ground and one of them grabbed a golf club and started smashing it. Then they went back inside and grabbed a bag of golf balls and started teeing them off at the windows of Unicol.

A guy pulled up outside the flat with a supermarket trolley tied to the back of his car. Another guy put on a skateboard helmet and hopped into the trolley and the car took off with him behind. He was laughing and screaming and rolling around. 'What the hell have I got myself into?' I thought. It was the perfect introduction to university life.

My parents had decided I was going to university in Dunedin. I wanted to go to Massey University, but I think my old man had given some thought to the challenge of making it in rugby while playing in a second-division union. He worked out that John Haggart, the first-five for Otago, was coming to the end of his career and decided I would have a better chance down there.

Chris Ellis: We sent him to Dunedin. There wasn't any modern collaborative thinking on that. He wanted to go to Massey because it was only a drive away from his girlfriend and home. There was every good reason why we didn't want that to happen. As an only child, we had to cut the cord. It was an opportunity for him to stand alone. He wouldn't be able to drive back at the weekends. We said to him, 'If you don't like it, you don't have to stay. Get on a plane and come home. But give it a go and have a crack.'

The whole process of getting to Unicol had been quite traumatic. I had to leave my girlfriend in Wellington and my folks for the first time, and when you're 18, that's a major.

Chris Ellis: The night before he went down there he was really quiet as we were packing his bags. There was a sense of unreality about it all.

I jumped on the plane and flew down to Dunedin on my own. It took about 40 minutes to drive in from Dunedin airport and in the mini-van I felt quite down. It was my first proper time away from home and I was a bit nervous.

Anne Ellis: He suffered a bit when he was little with homesickness, so that tempered all his invitations to stay with friends.

It was a bit of a gloomy, cloudy day, but finally the van came over the hill and I saw the expanse of the city open up before me. I could see Carisbrook, out to St Clair beach. Dunedin looked like a whole new world.

I wanted to live at Unicol but hadn't got in. Instead I was headed for Cumberland Hostel. Because I'd been a late applicant I was put in the nurses' quarters out the back, away from the rest of the hostel. It looked like an old mental asylum — plain white walls with bare beds in each eight-foot by 12-foot room. It was right by the road and I was homesick and missing my girlfriend. I was literally as low as I'd ever been in my life.

I decided to get off my chuff and do something, so I went for a walk down the main road, George Street. As I wandered along I was amazed at how everyone who walked past said gidday. I wondered if I looked like somebody else, because every 50 metres or so someone would say hello, but I later came to understand that was just how people were down there — they went out of their way to be friendly to the students. They could probably tell by the way I looked that I was a new recruit, a bit bright-eyed and bushy-tailed, and evidently they wanted to welcome me to Dunedin. It certainly cheered me up a bit.

I went to see Dr Rennie, the proctor of Unicol, to ask him why I hadn't been accepted there. He explained that my headmaster had written me a poor recommendation. Although I'd taken home fairly good reports while I was at Wellington College, he hadn't recommended me for Unicol. I was pretty disappointed about that. I felt like he'd stabbed me in the back (and years later, when I went back to Wellington College to do a speech, I had him up about it).

As luck would have it, a room had suddenly come up at Unicol and Dr Rennie offered it to me. I moved into room 514 in the south tower. The floors at Unicol had been integrated not long before I arrived, so I had eight girls and eight guys on my floor. Two of my mates from school — Johnny the Greek and Dave Bathgate — were on other floors. There were about 300 people altogether in the hostel, so I figured I had 150 potential mates, and 150 potential girlfriends, which was an exciting prospect.

Unicol was a fairly liberating place to be. We were all students for the first time in our lives, and free to make our own decisions. Nobody stood over you and made you work. I was paid an Away from Home student allowance of $134 a week, I got $50 a week from my parents, and I had my Mizuno sponsorship. I wanted for nothing. Three square meals were provided every day. I had nothing to worry about but going to lectures and having some fun.

There were all sorts of people. Some came from very privileged backgrounds, which I didn't; and some came from disadvantaged backgrounds, which I didn't either. I was from somewhere in the middle and I was keen to mix with everyone.

That first week was taken up with Orientation. It was a week of absolute mayhem and madness, a great icebreaker, and a precursor to the next five years. There were absurd hostel noise raids, where the folks from one hostel ran over to another and banged pots and pans outside — that didn't really light my candle — and huge parties and events with great New Zealand bands doing gigs.

Each of the five main hostels had a bath, a big old porcelain bath with the hostel's name written on it. It was an Orientation tradition that students from each hostel tried to steal the baths from other hostels. There was high security — first-years guarded the baths around the clock and bolt-cutters were needed to unchain them. The first night we went out stealing we were caught and dunked in a bath filled with ice-cold water. The next night Johnny the Greek, Dave Bathgate and I set out in the Greek's Nissan Sunny, a hatchback. We pounded the people protecting the baths with our weapon of choice, eggs, and were able to drag a bath into the boot and take off. We ended up with three baths that night.

Each floor at Unicol put on an Orientation skit, which was a great way to get everyone mixing and mingling. Me and a few other guys on my floor did a male ballet we called 'The Enchantment of the Bollock'. We wore girls' tights and leotards and frolicked across the stage. One guy was about two metres, another was 105 kilograms, and then there was me, so we were a sight to see. We had all the grace of a shot duck, so we were surprised when we won best skit.

After Orientation, classes started. I was enrolled in a marketing degree. I liked the idea of coming up with a message, designing a campaign, giving a product a look or a value, and accounting or finance, the other options, seemed too dry for me. My career plan was to get a marketing degree, become a sales rep, move up to sales manager and maybe become a marketing manager.

I quickly worked out that lectures weren't compulsory and if you found the person with the tidiest notes you could get by with having a good read of them at the end of the day. Of course, it didn't do the same job as sitting in a lecture hall listening to a teacher, but to be honest, having fun was my priority, then rugby, and then study. My philosophy was always 'C for comfort' — I did the bare minimum and scraped through. I never got an A; B+ was my highest mark because I didn't apply myself as I ought. Maybe that's why it took five years to finish my degree. Of course, if I went back now I would want to get straight As, but I don't regret my approach back then in the slightest. I was growing up and having fun and those years were some of the best in my life to date.

It didn't take long to make mates, and most of them are still my great mates to this day. We had a bloody good crew of guys and we had a ball. We quickly became desensitised to loose behaviour. We lived among 18,000 other students in the three-square-kilometre area of Scarfieville and it was a decadent frenzy of enjoying ourselves — just so much fun. It was all about making each other laugh and getting each other in a bit of trouble. Getting your mates to do something incredibly foolish and watching it happen — there's nothing better.

A lot of the time our pranks and high jinks involved drinking. That was a big part of the culture down there and it certainly loosened us up and led to some high-spiritedness. The Gardens Sports Tavern, Bar and Grill — the Gardies — became our local. It had a couple of beautiful pool tables (one of which I now own). We'd whip down there, play a few games of pool, have a few beers, and tell a few lies. The other student pubs, the Bowler, the Cook and the Oriental, would all have turns being popular, but we invariably returned to the Gardies.

One of our favourite tricks was to hide something really smelly in a mate's room, and leave it there to stink out the place. It got intense: you'd find a paper bag filled with something revolting clipped to your best shirt in the wardrobe, or under your mattress, or behind the heater in your room. There was one poor girl in the hostel who couldn't smell anything, so she was exploited somewhat. One of my best mates, Waffle, had a teddy bear on his bed that his girlfriend had given him to remember her by. It was wearing a handkerchief for a pair of shorts and that became a popular hiding place. His room absolutely stank. It was horrendous.

There wasn't a day that went by in Dunedin that there wasn't some sort of nude act. It was a great precursor to Nude Day and it was wholeheartedly embraced by all of the fellas. We'd quite often have a few beers at home in the nude, just for shits and giggles. Or go around to visit some of the other boys only to find them painting in the nick, floppy hats on their heads, or up to some other nonsense in the nude. Once, in that first year, I came out of the Cook with some friends and some pissed blokes we didn't know were dancing in the nude around some street signs they'd broken down and set on fire. It looked like fun, so we stripped off and jumped in. Until the cops arrived. Bolting nude from the police is an adrenalin rush that I would highly recommend, but the possible downside of being put in the holding cells in the nick is something to be avoided at all costs, I would imagine.

I set up my first business operation — mending doors in the hostel — fairly early on in 1991. It was a service in demand because people often had their doors kicked in by eager visitors, so I struck up a relationship with the on-site carpenter and convinced him that he didn't want to waste his time on such menial jobs. He gave me sandpaper, spray paint and glue, new barrels and locks, and I charged students $20 to replace their doors before they got in trouble with the proctor. It was brilliant. If I needed to drum up business, I had a few mates I could always point in the direction of a door or two of an evening, then I'd go and make a tidy profit the next day. By strange coincidence a lot of the pretty girls had their doors broken. Some of those jobs were very intricate and I made sure they took longer than they should to fix.

There were some lovely girls at Unicol. The best girls got snapped up fairly quickly, but the last thing I wanted in my first year was to get involved in another serious relationship. A lot of them got a thing we called 'Speight's arse' — a significant weight gain thanks to all that drinking and hostel food. They'd go home their first holidays and their mothers would be agog.

The unisex showers and toilets on each floor made for some interesting encounters. You could orchestrate being in the bathroom when a girl you liked was in there by working out what time her first lecture was. I often went along as my mate Murdoch's wingman so he could 'bump into' one particular girl: I'd stay out by the basins pretending to brush my teeth and cough when she walked in; that would be his sign to saunter out of a shower in a towel. It never worked for him, sadly, but God loves a trier.

Easter Tourney was a big deal in Dunedin. It was ostensibly a sporting event — Auckland, Massey, Victoria, Lincoln and Canterbury teams would compete — but basically it was just a massive hooley. In my first year it was in Otago, and before the teams even got there, there was trouble: some Massey students jumped off the Picton Ferry on the way south.

The Undie 500, a road trip from Lincoln University to Dunedin, happened the same weekend. The police escorted a convoy of Lincoln students down to Dunedin. Their cars all cost less than $500 and were decorated in very bad taste: there was one with a coffin on the roof called Ayrton Senna's Pit Crew; another called The Rolling Stone had a big tongue hanging out the back of it; others were strewn with condoms and lamb's wool (that really appealed to the Lincoln sense of humour) and various other things.

I got into the Otago team during my first year in Dunedin, which was pretty exciting. Training was on Tuesday and Thursday nights. There was so much competition for the spots in the side that I had to take training seriously and I could only go out one night a week, and that was after the game. Some people in the hostel were giving it a good lash three or four nights a week and I couldn't do that.

The night before University club games I'd sit in my room cooking my special Friday night dinner — lamb chops and grilled tomatoes — on the little grill Mum sent down to me, as the boys were getting themselves dolled up for the night out. Later on I'd be woken up at all hours by people banging and crashing as they came home, or by parties on the floor and in the common rooms. That was quite hard. One Friday night a group were having a real tally-ho outside my room. I came out and asked them to keep it down. Naturally they couldn't, so I grabbed my pillow and duvet and headed down to a mate's room to sleep on his floor. On the way a girl from another floor offered me her room, saying she'd crash out in mine when the party finished. I jumped into this tidy room that smelled nice and had a great kip. My room smelled awful given the aforementioned tactic of planting stinky objects, so the chance to have a night in a lady's room was such a treat.

My first year in the Otago team, we won the NPC title. I was absolutely shagged after that game. A spa was what I needed: the only place with a spa, and open at that late hour, was the local massage parlour so Waffle and I charged in.

The pool had a little slide and, as usual, we couldn't resist. We found some baby oil and starting whizzing up and down the slide. The ladies who worked there were quite flummoxed; they thought they were going to get some business and instead the customers were bobbing up and down in the pool like two greasy saveloys in a saucepan. It was a funny, funny evening and we definitely got our money's worth.

There were only two places to get food in Dunedin after a night out: Likely's takeaway bar or the 24-hour dairy. The owner of Likely's had a temper, especially after an hour or two of cheek from students. We'd come in after a night out and be mucking around jumping in the stainless fish tray at the front of the shop and flapping around like dying fish. The owner would retaliate by putting the hot chip scoop into the oil and flicking boiling-hot oil at us. He had to put up with a lot that guy, but having chip fat thrown at you wasn't nice. One of the things on his menu was deep-fried milk. It was sweetened condensed milk in batter, deep-fried. Rumour has it he picked one out of the fryer one night and threw it at a guy. It was like napalm. It exploded on impact and the burning hot condensed milk went through the guy's shirt as he went yelping out into the street like a wounded dog. The guy deserved it — he'd been drawing on the walls of the takeaway bar — but it must have tickled.

The 24-hour dairy saw plenty of action too; if the walls could talk in that place there'd be some stories for sure. The owners prosecuted anyone who shoplifted, even if it was for something as small as a K-bar, so a lot of people got done for shoplifting while at varsity. We regularly went home via The Two Four, and the receipts from there usually told us what time we'd got home.

Cars were of vital importance in Dunedin, a chance to show off your individuality and satisfy that little bit of bogan we all had in us. In those days people had flat cars — you'd all throw in some money and buy a car together, a big one that would fit everyone in it.

I didn't have a car in my first year, so I asked John Leslie if I could borrow his car — an old lime-green Kingswood — to collect Mum and Dad from the airport when they flew down for the first time. I turned up bright and early on a Saturday morning to borrow the car and it was hanging out of the front of his flat. The night before there had been a big party at JL's and some bright sparks had driven his car straight through the front of the house. Every bloody window in the car was broken. JL's solution was to sweep all the glass out of the car and hand over three ski jackets and three sets of ski goggles for me and my parents to wear. I turned up at the airport like that. Dad thought it was absolutely brilliant, but I'll never forget the look on Mum's face.

In my second year Waffle and I bought a 1971 Ford Falcon XY from Turner's auctions. She was a pretty special car, but our budget was $1200 and she was going to go for more than that, so we took her out for a test drive and changed all the plugs over so she started misfiring. We pushed her back into the garage and complained loudly that she was a dunger, and when she came up for auction we got her for a grand. She drove beautifully and took us on many a journey over the next 18 months, until Waffle blew her up on the way from Levin to Wellington.

We did lots of road trips with mates in those days and cars like my 1964 Falcon Deluxe station wagon were great because you could fold the seats down and sleep two comfortably. When we didn't have cars we'd hitch all over the country and I've met some bloody fine folk hitching.

In 1993 I got a yellow 1968 Valiant, the old square type. I was away with the All Blacks on a trip around Northland schools. We stopped at a pub in Kaiwaka and a girl in a singlet (with a fine array of tattoos) pulled up in this Valiant. I asked her what she wanted for it; we agreed on $250 upfront, and if the car made it back to Dunedin, another $500, which I'd send to her. The car didn't have a warrant or a rego, but I got her to Wellington and onto the Picton ferry, and when I made it to Dunedin I sent the remaining payment.

Two weeks later the bloody thing blew up, but she was great fun while she lasted. She was a beautiful car and had a really, really loud backfire every time she was turned off while going at about 50 km/h, which gave a lot of people a fright. I was driving out to Port Chalmers one day when we spied a guy on a pushbike. Naturally, we decided to drop a backfire on him, so as we passed I turned the car off and, with precision timing, my rear passenger pointed his hand out the window like a mock gun. The cyclist got such a fright he jumped off the bike and bolted off screaming. We took a different route home and packed in the backfire game for a while after that.

My mate Stu Velvin had a purple Cortina with fluffy dice. It was foul, but he looked great in it, probably because, like his car, Stu was a bit different.

Stu won a Skoda once, off the radio. He was so proud he drove it around to show the fellas. He came in the front door crowing about his new wheels and one of the boys kept him occupied while the others snuck out the back and tipped it on its roof and set it on fire! He came back outside and his car was alight. It was destroyed. Fortunately, Stu could see the humour in it.

Another example of our 'what's mine is mine and what's yours is mine too' attitude was the habit of 'borrowing' cars. Most people left the keys in their cars, so if we couldn't be bothered walking home from varsity or a mate's place we would just take a car, and leave it, with the keys still inside, at our final destination. The owner would find it — there were only a few streets to look down — and there was usually no harm done, but when one of my mates took it a step further and borrowed a taxi to get home from a 21st, it didn't end up so well. He got halfway there before he rolled the cab onto its roof. (He later argued that the taxi driver was inviting trouble by leaving the keys in the car, but I'm not sure about that.)

Swapping number plates was another great trick. We would unscrew someone's number plates, put them on our car, and then double-park it for a few days. Our mate would get a couple of hundred bucks' worth of parking tickets and have no idea how he got the fines.

We spent many a weekend hooning about. One friend acquired a fire engine from Turner's and about a dozen of us jumped on the back of it and drove up to Morningside where Gordy Hunter, my coach in the Otago team, lived, with the sirens going. Gordy came out yelling, 'Fire, fire!' We parked up and had a great afternoon round at his place. Another Sunday five of us bought a Humber wagon from an old hippie living south of Dunedin, and we spent the day driving it up to the top of the hill on Dundas Street, and racing back down in first gear, until it blew up. The van cost us $150, $30 each, a small price to pay for a whole day of fun.

The winters in Dunedin are long and cold and that first winter was a really bad one. In April there was so much rain that the Leith River, which runs through the middle of the university, flooded. Someone came up with the bright idea of tubing and we got some tractor inner tubes, threw them in, and jumped in the Leith. It was pretty hairy — when we went over the culverts we had to make sure we pushed ourselves out far enough to avoid getting sucked in by the water. One guy got sucked in and the fire brigade had to get him out. It was touch and go for a while there and that was our first warning that things could go wrong in that sort of environment. It didn't put us off playing silly buggers, though.

Plenty of injuries were sustained over the years — I could almost write a whole chapter on them. My friend Higgsy got into a few scrapes. He did a 'Dukes of Hazzard' roll over a moving car and got a windscreen wiper flush up his bull's-eye. The boys had to pry him off the windscreen and take him, bleeding, to the hospital to have the wound patched up. Trying to explain to the doctor what had happened was hilarious.

Higgsy was an unlucky bugger. On the night of the Melbourne Cup one year — and after collecting the trifecta — he attempted a running karate kick on the flat fence. He ended up with a groin full of 10-centimetre splinters and another trip to the hospital to have them extracted from his privates.

The closest call I ever had was in 1993. Jamie Joseph and Andy Rich needed a boat boy for a diving trip and I told them I had a bit of boating experience (which was a lie). The three of us drove about an hour north of Dunedin, just south of Oamaru, and launched the boat, an eight-foot inflatable with a six-horsepower Seagull motor on the back. If I had had a salty bone in my body I would have known it was a recipe for disaster: Jamie and Andy weighed at least 110 kilograms each, and we were all in this blow-up boat. We hadn't told anyone where we were going, or when we'd be back. None of us had lifejackets on.

When we got out about two kilometres offshore the guys tied the boat and me to a buoy and took off to pillage a few of the craypots. I did some fishing, but then the wind whipped up and it got very choppy. I could only see the pot that Jamie and Andy had gone down to when the boat hit the crest of a wave and I started to feel seasick.

Eventually the boys popped up and started waving, so I untied the boat and went to start it. That was a major screw-up on my part: you always start a boat before you untie it. The boat wouldn't start and I was rapidly heading south-east, off to Antarctica. I was desperately trying to get the motor going and I got the major shits on.

Twenty minutes later I finally got the motor into gear by removing its casing (risky if water splashes in I am told). By this time, though, I had well and truly lost sight of the guys. I knew they were clinging on to a craypot, but had no idea which one. I also knew that if they let go and tried to swim to safety they'd be swept out to sea.

I hit on a good idea: I had been squinting into the sun when I was tied to the craypot, so I figured if I followed the sun back in, I should hit it again. I went a bit further out to sea, along the coast, then followed the sun in, in a straight line. Ten minutes passed and I still couldn't see them, so I decided to go straight to shore and call the coastguard.

On the way in I spied them. They'd dropped their gear, their weight belts, their catch bags (full of crayfish), everything. The two of them didn't know whether to beat me up or kiss me. Once we got back to shore we drove straight to the pub and sat in absolute silence having a beer. (That weekend I got a worried phone call from my old man: 'What the hell is this I hear about you bloody nearly losing your life in a diving accident?' he said. I hadn't told him or Mum about it because I knew they would fret, but one of the TV commentators had mentioned it during that week's Otago game.)

Looking back on stories like that now, I realise it's a wonder that I came out unscathed. No wonder my parents worried.

* * *

In the Christmas holidays that year I got a job working at O'Reilly's, a big bottle store owned by Zuk Marinkovich in Wellington. I had worked there during the school holidays the year before and some of my mates worked there too. We got paid a pittance, but enough to go on a summer holiday at the end of it, and there was always the chance of extra work, waitering at the various Christmas parties for which Zuk supplied the booze. That was pretty big news for us — we got to go to these fancy parties and sneak the odd drink while we were on the job.

Some of my friends' little brothers worked in the O'Reilly's warehouse too. We made them do all the hard work whenever possible. One kid in particular was a cheeky little bugger and when he refused to do something one day we grabbed him and dragged him into the freezer. We bound and gagged him with his hands and his legs behind his back and put duct tape over his mouth, and left him there. An hour and a half later Zuk went ripping into the freezer looking for some chilled wine and found the kid shivering in the corner. I was already in the bad books: a few days earlier I'd driven the delivery van too close to a pallet and taken the door off. And I'd stuffed the forklift by bending the forks back on the ceiling. Zuk was renowned for his temper, so I knew there was going to be major trouble. Luckily, our victim didn't dob us in, and I denied it, pretending to be shocked and disappointed that anyone would contemplate such an atrocious trick.

I always looked forward to coming home to Wellington and catching up with my friends from school. One of my mates, James Churchward (known as Cookie) would go to the gym with me most days I was in town. Cookie and I had made the Wellington Colts rugby team together in our last year at Wellington College. He was a guy who we all thought would be an All Black. He was robust around the field, incredibly fit and strong, the sort of guy who had the potential to at the very least play provincial rugby very well.

When we all went away to varsity Cookie stayed in Wellington and in 1992 he committed suicide. That was one of the biggest blows, to hear that my dear mate had taken such a drastic step. There were no signs at all; none of us had any idea that the guy was going through a tough time. Trying to work out what we all could have done to help him was bloody hard. If only he had reached out and told someone how brassed off he was with life — we would have had an opportunity to help him. That's what friendship's all about. Farewelling a friend at that age, that's a prick of a thing.

A Fair Few Distractions

Towards the end of my year in Unicol, we all started to work out who we wanted to flat with next year. I wanted to live with my mates and, ideally, also wanted to rope in a couple of girls, preferably girls who had high standards of cleanliness — if their tolerance for filth was low, we could be sure they'd keep the place clean. (The downside to that was once we moved in, the girls invariably got angry about the mess.) If you chose the right girls, they didn't eat much — Sesameal crackers with cheese and chutney rather than too many carbs or meat. The boys, on the other hand, would come home after a couple and hoover up whatever was left in the fridge and cupboards. It also helped to pick the least glamorous girls you knew: that way you wouldn't be tempted to break the golden rule of flatting — 'Don't Screw the Crew'.

The primary concern was location; the proximity to varsity, Castle and Dundas Streets, and the pubs in town. We wanted a house on its last legs because we didn't want to pay much more than $50 a week each (and so any incidental damage would be hard to spot). Organised students, The Analists, as we called them, started flat-hunting well in advance, sometimes in the March of the year before. We left it to the last moment, which guaranteed the worst of flats and that is how seven of us ended up in 'Footrot Flats'.

Footrot Flats was a fairly well-known flat in Scarfieville and even though it should have been condemned we fell in love with it. It was a two-storey house with tatty industrial carpet and poorly painted walls. The toilet was at the back, almost outside.

Picking rooms was always a bloody difficult process in flats. All sorts of techniques were employed. One strategy was to get down there before anyone else and just set yourself up in the best room. Then there was the straw pull. I got the second to worst room in Footrot Flats, thanks to the old straw pull. It was freezing in the winter and I had only an old fan heater for warmth. The thermostat on the heater was stuck on −3°C, so it would come whirring into life only when it got that cold, which was invariably 1 a.m. It's no wonder some couples got together only for the winter months, just to keep warm.

Johnny the Greek got a first-floor bedroom and we could climb out his window, sit on the roof and get a glimpse of the afternoon sun. We were sitting out there one day, enjoying a cleansing ale, when we noticed a bloke walking up the hill in a black suit. He looked lost, so we called out. That was all the encouragement he needed; he came up on the roof and quickly launched into a well-rehearsed prattle about the Book of Mormon. After five long minutes of him selling us on the Mormon faith I was contemplating jumping off the roof. Then we started to have some fun with our new friend, telling him that our flatmate Dave would be bitterly disappointed to have missed his visit and perhaps he could leave some books for him. The guy started salivating like a rabid dog and came back once a week, trying to convert Dave to the faith. I think he even tracked Dave down in his new flat the following year.

The neighbours' flat was condemned while we lived at Footrot Flats. It was in an awful condition to be sure, but no worse than our place. The occupants were a bit more cunning than us, though. They called the Health Department, claiming the property was riddled with rats. Before an inspector came to have a look they shot off to the pet shop and bought a bag of rodents, which they let loose. The ruse worked and the landlord received a demolition order. The tenants offered the landlord a reduced rent of $15 a week, which he accepted — as the saying goes, 'adversity breeds genius'.

We all lived on a fairly tight budget in those days. My mate Pee Wee, who was at Wellington College with me, didn't have enough money to go into a flat so he offered friends $15 a week for their woodshed. He bought himself a second-hand waterbed and shoved it in there. It took up the entire shed and was wedged in — if you went to visit him you had no choice but to lie on the bed. To keep warm Pee Wee kept the mattress up quite hot (he ran an extension cord out from the house for power) and nailed Pink Batts to the walls of the shed. Eventually, in the dead of the winter, the heater in the waterbed broke and the water in it froze solid. Pee Wee couldn't move the bed out because it was a massive block of ice so he hammered wood over the mattress, put down a layer of Pink Batts, then some bedding, and slept on that.

To pay his rent Pee Wee started a fruit-and-vege run. He signed flats up for a $20 bag each week and then he went and got the ugly off-cuts of fruit and vege, bagged them up and made his deliveries. It was a great idea — it saved everyone going to the supermarket for their greens — but he had reliability issues so we could never be sure when we'd have veges to go with our meat.

Some of my mates had a real eye for a financial opportunity. In 1992 the Otago team went up to Canterbury for a Ranfurly Shield challenge. We had beaten them in the pre-season, and the year before, and everyone thought we were going to take the shield. Entrepreneurs that they were, Chiz and Sniff hit on the idea of getting 1000 T-shirts printed with 'The Shield Belongs in the House of Pain'. Their plan derailed when, due to logistical problems, the T-shirts didn't arrive from the printers until the Monday after the match. By that time everyone in New Zealand knew that Otago had lost. The boys went door to door around Dunedin trying to sell the T-shirts at a discounted rate, and there are probably still plenty left if anyone's interested.

That same weekend my best mate Simon (who was at Lincoln University at that stage) and Waffle (who had hitched up from Dunedin) hopped in a cab to come and watch the game at Lancaster Park. They started a conversation with the taxi driver, expertly manipulating the conversation around to the midfield clash, with the hope that my name would pop up. As soon as the taxi driver said my name, the fun began. 'Of course, you know Marc lives in Dunedin in a one-bedroom apartment with another guy,' they said. They thought it was a great joke, spinning that yarn, and carried it on for the entire taxi ride. They reckon that by the time they got out of the car they'd done a good job of convincing the taxi driver that I was an overt homosexual. Encouraged by the taxi driver's response, they carried on the same story with every taxi driver they met that weekend. I still get the odd strange look from cabbies in the Garden City.

Meanwhile, two other friends, up from Dunedin, found themselves lost and cold after a big night out wandering the suburbs of Christchurch. Finding a side window open at a random house, they climbed in and helped themselves to the spare beds. The next morning they were woken by a woman, saying, 'You must be some of Johnny's mates. Come on, breakfast is ready.' The boys put on their poker faces and trotted out for bacon and eggs. They had a job pulling it off as they were cross-examined over the breakfast table by Johnny's younger brother, who smelt a rat. One of the boys took him aside for a quiet chat and they made their escape full up and unexposed.

In those days the Lord's Day of Rest invariably turned into something quite special. The pubs opened, but you had to eat food (the law didn't really make any sense at all, but it was a lovely loophole), so we'd buy a cheap toasted sandwich at the Gardies and then sit there all day and have a few jars. Every now and then, after a Sunday session, we would embark on what was known as the Castle Street Mile. All we needed was a big sack and our mate the Tongan Yam, who was an expert at the 'Mile'. We'd charge down the street booting in the back doors of flats and raiding our mates' fridges. Traditionally, the flat shopping was done on a Sunday so there was usually plenty to nick. We'd get home with frozen chickens, kilos of mince, four or five bags of bread, tomatoes, lettuces, lots of milk (you didn't bother with the eggs obviously as they'd break on the way home). We didn't look on it as thieving — that 'what's yours is mine' philosophy again — and the next Sunday someone would usually do the same to our place.

Food was sometimes a scarce resource and there were many ingenious ways of obtaining it for free. I had mates who lived right on the Leith. They had a plentiful supply of duck and, at the right time of year, spawning salmon. The ducks were lured into the woodshed with bread and were then made short work of (as an animal lover I didn't ask too many questions about what went on in there, but I have to concede I did enjoy the odd roast duck). Catching salmon was easier and involved the use of a butterfly net and a baking dish. Other friends frequented Amway sales meetings, where there was a sort of wine and cheese evening with a presentation in the middle. Suffice to say no one joined the sales team but they all left with a glow on and some camembert in their pockets.

Romance in Dunedin was difficult. There weren't many opportunities to do something romantic, a special night out. A video and a trip to the Alcala Motor Lodge, where they had a spa pool, was about as good as it got. You could book their Grotto (a spa with a few plants and little fairy lights around it) for an hour, but in the interests of hygiene it paid to make sure you were one of the first to go there of a weekend.

Coldstarts were popular among our crew. A coldstart dinner meant that every guy in the flat had to invite a girl they'd never met before to dinner (and vice versa for the girls in the flat). It was a big event in the social calendar, a bulk blind date, and the impetus for it was usually that someone had spotted a rather special girl around varsity and wanted to ask her out. The date would be set, then we would have to go out and ask a girl along, which was pretty nerve-wracking because you'd have to sell yourself to a complete stranger in a couple of sentences.

The night of the coldstart we'd go and collect our dates dressed in our Number Ones — moleskins, RM Williams boots. Usually our only wheels were the flat car, so we'd all pile in together and pick the girls up, in one, sometimes two, trips. Back at the flat, there were all sorts of games to break the ice, like Pass the Jetplane (where you passed it in your mouth to the girl sitting next to you), and compulsory tequila slammers, with the salt licked from behind the ear of the girl to your left. The boys would cook a lamb roast and splash out on a couple of bottles of wine.

Invariably, there'd be one girl who was the hit of the party, which would result in all the guys feverishly trying to get on-side with her.

The old saying, 'Never judge a book by its cover', was never more appropriate than in that environment. There were always bolters.

I became ineligible for coldstarts halfway through my second year because I started going out with Mandy Smith. Mandy had been in Unicol the same year as me — in fact she was the first person I spoke to in Unicol, over lunch on the day I moved in — but our friendship didn't turn into anything else until 1992. We had a lot in common — she was playing top-level hockey and I was playing rugby — so we understood each other's lifestyles. We had a lot of fun together too. We'd get away from varsity every now and then and go to her folks' place in Central Otago, which was cool. Ranfurly and the Maniototo is a boomer spot. The road through the Pig Route is still my favourite road in New Zealand. Coming down into the Maniototo off the hills is a stunning drive.

I hadn't been seeing Mandy long when I went to her 21st. It was fancy dress and at her Mum and Dad's place. I went as Elvis and it was a cracker night.

The next day her brother John invited me to the local tavern for a drink. I knew he wanted to size me up, so we went off to the pub for the afternoon and played some darts. We made a rule that the loser of each game had to skull a drink. John lost the first game and refused; eager to impress, I had it for him. Every time he lost, I drank for him; every time I lost I drank for myself.

Four or five hours later I was dropped back at Mandy's parents' house. Needless to say I could barely stand. I'd been well and truly stitched up by her brother. I looked a mess — my shoes were on the wrong feet — and things were about to get much worse; so bad that it hurts me to even tell this story, it's so humiliating.

I got inside the house and there, waiting in the lounge to meet me, were some old friends of the Smiths (I believe they were rather religious). Very quickly Mandy's mum said, 'Mandy, put Marc to bed'. Mandy escorted me into the spare bedroom, stripped me, put me in the bed, and left me to sleep it off.

I woke up an hour or so later feeling very unwell. I raced to the window to be sick. There was a fly-screen over it that I couldn't open so, panicking, I bolted, in my boxers, not knowing what I was doing, through the lounge, past Mandy's parents and their friends, into Mr and Mrs Smith's room, where I was very ill. Mandy found me passed out in the shower a few minutes later. It was so embarrassing and a few hours later I had to face the Smiths and say my farewells before we headed back to Dunedin. It was hardly the impression a young man wants to make on his new girlfriend's parents, but fortunately Mandy's parents gave me another chance and I was accepted by the Smith clan.

Mandy and I were together for a great seven years, but in hindsight it was not something that was going to last forever. When we broke up there was a lot of speculation and conjecture about us. I didn't want to discuss it publicly then and I don't want to go into it in any depth now either, except to say it was the right decision for us to make — a mutual decision — and a toughie for the pair of us. Afterwards, life went on. When I heard she was seeing Dean Barker I was thrilled, and I think it's great that Mandy's a wife and mum now.

Nineteen ninety-two was the year for 21sts amongst my crew and there were some real hooleys in Dunedin. My 21st was at the Wharf Hotel, an old sailors' hangout. My old man gave me a couple of bucks to put on some savouries and Lion Breweries helped me out with a few beers. The theme was fancy dress — you had to come as your hero. We had bogans, rastas, all sorts. It was a great night.

A mate over from Queenstown for the party arrived and handed me my birthday present, a little brown kunekune piglet in a sack. The pig was let loose and spent most of the night running around the pub and at the end of the night I took it home to the flat in a taxi. The poor thing was shivering, probably cold and scared, so I brought it into my bedroom to sleep for the night and let it out of the sack.

I woke up the next morning to a thumping coming from underneath the bed. I stuck my head over the side and there was this little pig snuffling in my face. My room stunk to high heaven. In the night Szusty (as he'd been named, after a Jewish mate) had jumped on my desk and eaten an entire chocolate cake a friend had made me for my birthday. He had then proceeded to defecate throughout my room.

I put Szusty back in the sack and moved him to my flatmate Waffle's room for the rest of the morning. (Waffle woke up with a hazy recollection of the events of the night before and found a writhing sack at the foot of his bed.) Gordy Hunter came around later that day and tied Szusty to the clothesline by his back legs. Forty-eight hours later his back leg was just about turning blue because the rope was so tight so I decided to make him a hutch. We ripped the back door and some palings off the back of the house and made Szusty a nice home, but the little bugger rooted his way out every day and escaped down the road. We'd have to go around the neighbourhood asking people if they'd seen a pig, and bring him back.

By this stage the winter had well and truly come and Szusty was suffering from the cold, so we gave up on the hutch and put him in the downstairs bathroom, making him a nest in the bath. Szusty loved that — Johnny the Greek used to shower with him, and we would open the bathroom door and hurl in scraps for him to devour — but the girls in the flat did not. The bathroom was a mess and Szusty was putting on weight at an alarming rate, and eventually he had to go. A little kid took him and fattened him up on his farm and I was so grateful to him for giving Szusty a good home.

Szusty got up to 90 kilograms before he was slaughtered. We got 20 kilograms of bacon and about 40 kilograms of roasts and chops out of him. We had to buy a new chest freezer for all the meat. Midway through the next year, we still had heaps of meat to get through when the varsity holidays came around. We all buggered off for a few weeks, no one paid the power bill, and our service was cut off. When I got back to the flat I could smell the freezer from the front door — it was full of rotting meat. We dragged the freezer outside and, with the aid of a little petrol, torched it. It still stunk something chronic so I paid a guy who knew how to lose things a dozen Speight's to remove it. I watched in horror as he tied the freezer to the tow bar of his car with its power cord, then floored it off down Dundas Street. When he dropped a sharp right into Castle Street, the cord snapped and the freezer flipped head over tail down the road, spewing its contents.

I was at a fantastic party at JL's the night I got arrested for being drunk in charge of a motor vehicle. It was a fancy dress do and everyone had to come as someone in particular, as decided by JL: Arran Pene was the Incredible Hulk, Stu Forster was a garden gnome, JL's flat came as the Jackson 5 and I was Fonzie. I had stove-pipe jeans, winkle-pickers, leather jacket, my hair slicked back. Two guys came as Ponch and John from 'CHiPs' and they arrived on their nifty-fiftys, which they rode into the party.

Someone suggested the Fonz should do a lap of the Octagon, which sounded like a bloody good idea at the time. Two years before, when I got DIC'd in Wellington, I had vowed never to drink and drive again because it's such a stupid thing to do, but I didn't even think about being DIC'd on a moped. I hopped straight on the bike and drove into the lift (the party was at a fourth-floor apartment) then down and out into the Octagon. It was about 1 a.m. and I rode around so slowly I could have picked the bike up and jogged with it faster. Then I heard the sirens go on and I thought, 'Oh shit, I'm going to be in trouble for this'.

The cop was a woman and one of those types who are pissed off about it. She marched over and asked my name and in an attempt to defuse the situation with a bit of humour I went, 'Aye', with the thumbs up like the Fonz. That went down poorly and I knew this was all going to blow up in my face.

The policewoman took me down to the police station, where I asked to make a phone call to my dad (I wanted to call him to obtain the name of an appropriate lawyer as I had no idea who to phone to represent me). I wasn't allowed to make the call and in court the judge ruled that my rights had been breached by the refusal of that phone call. The case was thrown out. Sadly, though, the police took it to the High Court and I was disqualified from driving for three months and got 100 hours of community service. To this day Crown vs. Marc Ellis is case law in New Zealand and I am not terribly proud of that. I must concede, however, that I laughed to myself about the absurdity of the whole thing. Personally, I think it should have been handled with a kick in the arse and the keys being taken — but that's probably why I'm not a cop.

However, I learnt once and for all that you're a moron if you drink and drive and I learnt that it's not just cars and motorbikes you can be DIC'd on: it's nifty-fiftys, push bikes and horses. I also learnt that going away on a school camp is the best way of doing community service: I went off for four days and nights and served it all at once. It's something to keep in mind if, like me, you're likely to get into a spot of bother.

* * *

A lot of students were so shell-shocked by their first experience of flatting in Dunedin that they moved out of Scarfieville in their third year and out to North East Valley, about 20 minutes' walk from varsity. It was an alternative lifestyle out there — a lot of crushed velvet was being worn. Others went out to live at the beach, even further away. Neither would have worked for me as I'm a notoriously poor timekeeper and getting to lectures on time would have been even more difficult than usual.

In 1993 I moved to a house in Castle Street with JL, Waffle and Dave Bathgate. We went for something a bit more upmarket and stylish than Footrot Flats. Bob Marley took pride of place on our Hero Wall in the lounge. I love Bob Marley, he's one of my idols, and I love his music so we always had some good reggae sounds going down.

Our social rugby team was named The Wailers in Bob's honour and everyone had number 35 on their jersey because we thought Bob Marley died when he was 35. He actually died when he was 36 so we screwed that up, but all having the same number served a purpose. One evening, after a Wailers game, one of the players known as the Ginger Abo flogged a pie and did a runner while wearing his rugby jersey. He was reported to the police for the theft, but as we all wore the same number on our jerseys, it was too hard for them to pin it on him (despite his unusual look).

Our flat was 100 metres from the Gardies and afforded an unparalleled view of the talent coming and going from the pub. My bedroom was right on the road, so I'd hear people leaving the pub every night. Beer bottles would be smashed outside, and I'd hear people running up and over the top of cars parked on the street and I learnt to sleep like a rock. We had a lovely old lady living next door, one of the half dozen residents in Scarfieville who wasn't a student. She must have been hard of hearing, or a superb sleeper, because she didn't ever complain about the noise.

In 1991 and 1992 I had had a fair few distractions (primarily social rather than sporting) and I hadn't done so well at varsity. In fact, I think I got three papers in two years. So it was no surprise when I got a letter saying I had to toe the line and get all my papers in 1993 or I was going to be kicked out.

I hated studying. For me it was a mental trauma — I would have preferred physical punishment, being stretched on a rack, to studying for an exam — but I did put my head down and do a bit of work after my warning. I also did a fair bit of cheating.

In our first year a couple of the boys and I came up with a great trick. We scoped out the best students in the marketing class, the ones who took the best notes, and waited till we could see them sitting in their hostel room studying. We then set the fire alarm off. If you started the fire alarm and got caught, you got a fine, so it was a risky manoeuvre but one that paid off. While everyone was standing outside waiting for the fire engines, we'd nab the notes left behind and run down to the photocopier in the office, where we'd copy them. For free! Then we'd get the notes back on the right desk before everyone came back inside.

One time we broke into the Commerce building and, using a ruler with a bit of chewing gum stuck on the end of it, fished out assignments from the tutorial boxes. We photocopied the good ones and then copied bits of them into our essays. One of our mates, Chesney, would never give us any help on our marketing assignments. He'd say he hadn't even started the assignment when he'd already handed it in.

In exams, if I sat one row behind and one seat to the right of a smart-arse, I could usually copy their multi-choice answers. In maths exams I would write formulae out on the back of my calculator in pencil, which couldn't be seen except in the right light.

Another trick was to forge parts of the marketing textbooks and then hide them in a completely foreign area of the library where they would be hard to find (for checking), but the best cheat I ever did was in Physiology of Sport. Every year the exam had the same essay options, so I took some additional paper out of another exam the week before and wrote the physiology essays on it at home beforehand. In the exam I just pulled out the extra paper and stuck it in my test booklet.

Our cunning tricks were nothing compared to the skills used by a guy who was infamous for his aegrotat degree. The bloke, a Lincoln student I met a few times, hated exams so much he decided to get his degree entirely by aegrotat, without ever sitting an exam. And he went to any length to swing it. In his first year, just before exams, he got friends to hit him on the hands with phone books, in an attempt to break his fingers. That didn't work so he resorted to slamming a car boot on his digits, which eventually rendered him unable to write. The next year he used a cheese grater on his face, ran his bike over with his car, and called an ambulance, claiming he'd been hit by a car. He missed his exams because of suspected concussion. In his third year the guy left a dead chicken on the doorstep in the sun for a couple of days and then drank its blood in the hope he'd get salmonella. Sure enough, 72 hours later, he was crook as. The guy was a legend; without any exams, he had an extra month's holiday each year.

In between lectures it was always nice to have a wander down George Street for a look in the shops and a coffee at Modacks. One of the fantastic things about Dunedin is that there are a huge number of freaks per capita and you were guaranteed to come across one or two while out walking. There was Speedy, who used to walk around holding a transistor radio to the side of his head. Speedy, so rumour has it, walked the entire Dunedin bus route every day, a huge distance. He was quite relaxed, until he was crossed, and if anyone flogged his radio, which I saw happen once, Speedy would put on one of the most ferocious displays of aggression ever witnessed.

Joan the Butcher was not really a butcher, but she was pretty fruity. Hairy Guy was a redhead who wore a possum-skin vest and a pair of jeans. It didn't matter if it was −5°C with a wind chill, or 25°C and scorching hot, this guy would only wear a possum-skin vest, his big hairy ginger chest proudly on display. Triangle Man used to pull his pants up really high. He was shaped like a triangle and he wore Roman sandals and had a beautiful comb-over hairdo. Tricycle Guy wore a black suit like an undertaker and rode a kid's tricycle around town.

We had a mate who called himself Unit Man. He was a hell of a good bugger. He used to call the police and report an idiot riding a motorbike recklessly in the Octagon, then rush down there on his motorbike and pull wheelies and donuts. When the police arrived he'd burn off. Another one of his tricks was to jump out of second-floor windows and onto the roof of a parked van.

On a good day there would be buskers out on George Street and one day JL and I came across a guy juggling fire. He was going pretty poorly to be fair — he kept dropping his fire sticks — and there wasn't a lot of money in his hat, so we offered him $10 if he would eat some fire. It was a big ask, as he clearly didn't have the skill set for fire-eating, but he took it on. He lifted the fire stick to his face, leaned back, and instantly drips of the hot flaming jelly wax fell on his chin. It was like getting a triple flaming Sambuca wrong — his face went up like a Roman candle and he had to dash off very quickly and roll himself in a blanket. It's probably the hardest $10 that guy has ever earned in his life (and one of the best I've spent).

In 1994 I moved into a brilliant house on Gore Place with four other guys. It was the corner property and tradition dictated it was the site for a big party every year, so we happily co-ordinated that. In fact there were lots of parties at Gore Place. We basically used it as a party venue and went to our girlfriends' places, where it was clean and nice, to sleep. In the middle of winter, it was so cold at Gore Place that as we sat watching TV we'd pull off the wallboards and stick them in the fire. By the time we left there the lounge was poked.

I lived in Dundas Street in 1995. Even though it was my fifth year at varsity, most of my friends were still in Dunedin as well. It wasn't that we didn't want to finish in three years, but we were just having that much fun. I've always been a bit of a Peter Pan anyway. I've never been in a hurry to grow up and grow old and have a lot of responsibility. I reckon you've got to enjoy your childhood and long may it last. There are too many 13-year-olds these days acting as if they're 20. That's a shame because the innocence of youth is great. It should be enjoyed as long as humanly possible, I believe.

I went back to Dunedin in 1996 to graduate. That was a cracker weekend. I was with the Warriors by then, but I'd had it put in my contract that I could have the weekend of my graduation off because there was no way I was going to miss it.

At the graduation ceremony Judith Medlicott, the chancellor of the university, presented the degrees. I'd been to a party for her niece at Judith's house in Maori Hill once. She had given me a lecture about choosing between sport and university that night and I needed a drink or two to recover afterwards. Predictably, a few of us really got out of control. There was a big glasshouse out the back with a pool in it and a few of the boys stumbled across pairs of Judith's togs and jumped into them — two of them in one pair at one stage. Eventually, the whole party ended up in the pool. It was complete chaos. It went down really poorly, so I made sure I gave Judith a big smile as she handed over my degree.

After graduation I went, with 10 of my mates, their parents and mine, to a restaurant for dinner. That group of mates, The Tight 10 as we call ourselves, mean the world to me. I know most of those mates would take a bullet for each other. The friendships we made in those varsity years are enduring, largely because of all those silly nights and high jinks we enjoyed. Dinner that night was an opportunity for us to farewell the varsity days on our own terms once and for all.

I go back to Dunedin every year or so now, and a lot of the old flats have been torn down to make room for apartments. They don't have the character of the houses I lived in, but I guess they make for a better investment, and the heart of Dunedin, that Scarfie way of life, is still intact. You don't find that in any other university campus in New Zealand. When I chat to kids about what they're going to do after school, I always suggest they go to Dunedin. It really worked for me. I loved it down there. It was one of the coolest times of my life. And I left there with a piece of paper saying I wasn't as silly as some might have thought.

Vintage Rugby

It was only a couple of weeks after I moved to Dunedin in 1991 that club rugby trials started. I was torn between trying out for the Otago Varsity Senior A side, or for the Under-21 team, known as the Varsity Blues (the next team down). The senior A side was the best in the club, but the Varsity Blues team was where a lot of people, including the likes of Taine Randell and Anton Oliver in later years, started out, and a team from which a number of Otago players had been picked without playing senior rugby at all. Both teams played vintage rugby — throwing the ball wide, running it from anywhere — and that was all I ever wanted to do at school. In the end I decided to go for Varsity A; it was a bigger challenge, but I thought, 'Bugger it, I'll have a crack'.

The trial was pretty nerve-wracking. I was playing against grown men. But I backed myself. My fitness was pretty high. I'm sure all those Friday-night runs to my girlfriend's house helped, but I was also lucky because I was small, so I retained my fitness a bit longer than some of the big boys I knew. I could have a month off and a summer holiday away with the boys, having a few beers every day, and I'd be OK.

I was always one of the fittest guys in any team because I had the philosophy that if I'd done more work than the guy I was marking I could back my skills to get me through.

John Leslie, Otago centre, ex-flatmate: John Campbell, AKA The Masochist, came over to Marc at the trials and said, 'You'll be alright mate, don't be nervous'. Marc's response was, 'I know. Don't worry about me mate, just make sure you do your own bloody job.'

When the team was named I was put into Varsity A at first-five. The manager of the team misread my name on the list and called me Mac instead of Marc. That turned into Macca, and the nickname's stuck. Later Earle Kirton christened me Lush (because he knew I had a good thirst).

John Leslie: He's also known as Divide by 10 and Getaway Driver. Divide by 10 because he likes to do a bit of colouring-in with the stories he tells — if you divide his stories by 10, you get somewhere close to the truth. Getaway Driver refers to the one or two times he was quite literally the getaway driver — enough said.

The University club had had more All Blacks than any other club in New Zealand in those days. We had an amazing side — a forward pack that was the equal of any other pack in New Zealand club rugby. The loose trio was Arran Pene, Tony Hunt and Josh Kronfeld, and the tight five all represented Otago too. In the backline we had the likes of John Timu and John Leslie. The fun we had playing for that club was unparalleled.

I spent five years playing for University. We didn't win every game, but we won the competition every year. Every week the 'Bloody Scarfies' were the team everyone wanted to knock over. We were pretty cocky; we weren't tested too often in games, so we were pretty confident in our abilities and didn't take it too seriously. Before a semi-final against Southern once, the call came out to wear Hawaiian shirts and gold chains. We arrived at the field dressed in Hawaiian shirts, big gold medallions, looking like pimps. It must have unsettled the opposition to see us swaggering around, but it also had the effect of ensuring we played well. You simply can't turn up dressed like that and lose.

In my first season I was picked for the New Zealand Colts team and the New Zealand University side too. Jock Hobbs, my old Wellington hero, coached the university side and that's where I had my first run at centre.

Jock Hobbs: I asked him to go to centre because we had another capable first-five. He was always willing to do what was in the best interests of the team. He was a very, very capable first-five, but he played very well at centre in that game.

I wore headgear for that first game at centre. (I'd been knocked out in club rugby the week before by some prop, who had booted me in the bonce on his way to a ruck, and as I came to I had been very confused. I couldn't understand why I was wearing a light-blue jersey, rather than a black Wellington jersey, and when I spied the sand dunes beside Dunedin's Tahuna Park I assumed I was playing somewhere on the Kapiti Coast, just out of Wellington. I'd completely forgotten I'd moved to Dunedin.) It was a mid-week game against the New Zealand A team and I was marking Bernie McCahill, who was a current All Black. It was my first opportunity to mark someone from the team I dreamt of being in one day, and I was wearing a bright-blue helmet, which was pretty embarrassing. (In those days it was thought that headgear stopped players from being KO'd; in reality all it prevented was head wounds.) As it happened I scored University's only try that day, which was a buzz, but just to have held my own in that game was a real confidence booster.

Jock Hobbs: Marc was, along with several other Otago players, the backbone of the Universities side. He was a very talented player and versatile, but intelligent and good fun too. University rugby has its own culture, one that's maybe a little more tolerant of personalities. There was good humour, a lot of fun. When work needed to be done, it was done.

John Hart was the Colts coach. I was excited about playing for him — he was a great coach, who always had time for the players, and a nice chap. He took the team to Invercargill for a game, my first at centre for the Colts. We went out and beat the Aussies by about 60 points. It was a cracker.

A few days before that game John put me in charge of the entertainment committee, which had to organise something to keep us out of trouble the evening before the game. I suggested go-karting. John lambasted me for choosing such a dangerous sport and said no.

I thought he was being way too anal and I told him he was wrong, that there was no risk associated. My call got vetoed.

A year or so later, the day before an All Blacks trial in Rotorua, we went go-karting. Mark Cooksley, who must be about seven feet tall, almost needed Sunlight soap and a shoehorn to get into the kart. When he finally got on the track he went flying around a corner and got clipped from behind by one of the other boys. He shot off and, being such a big man, went straight through the barrier of tyres. He didn't stop until he slammed into a closed roller door at about 30 km/h. He blew the bottom of the door up and was wedged underneath it: All you could see was his head and torso; his legs and feet and most of the go-kart were through the other side. The poor bugger skinned his shins and almost took his kneecaps off. He was yelping and we couldn't get the automatic door to go up, so eventually we had to lift it off him. Dear old John Hart was bang on about go-karting!

Before long I'd had a few good games for Varsity A and had got the odd good write-up in the paper. I began to think that I could play on the wing for Otago if I was given the chance and it wasn't long before that opportunity presented itself.

Earle Kirton: When Marc went to Otago I followed his progress. By April or May that year I said to Laurie, 'Have you grabbed that kid Ellis yet? If you don't grab him, I'll speak to his father about getting him back to Wellington. He's a bit of a creampuff, a lush, but he's too good really.' Laurie laughed and two weeks later Marc was in the Otago squad.

Laurie Mains, ex-All Black, ex-Otago coach, ex-All Blacks coach: He had a bit of a reputation as an exciting player so I watched him several times in club rugby and decided to bring him into the Otago team because of his flair. Earle only spoke to me about Marc as a first-five but it was going to be very difficult for him to get that spot for Otago, so in 1991 he played on the wing and he showed incredible talent and brilliance at times.

I was first called into the Otago team to be a reserve in a pre-season game against Southland. Tony Fordray, who played in the Under-21

Varsity Blues team, was picked ahead of me to play on the wing — proof of the breeding ground the Blues team was and is — while I got picked to be a back reserve (because I was versatile enough to play in a few positions, I think).

Fortunately, I didn't get onto the field in that game, because I was in bad shape. Laurie Mains, the Otago coach, had stumbled across the idea of caffeine-loading. He thought it might be the next big thing for sports players and told us to have a strong cup or two of coffee, with a couple of teaspoons of instant coffee in them, before the game. I had never drunk coffee in my life, and assumed the more the merrier, so I put six teaspoons of coffee in my cup and forced it down. I had a second one and it wasn't long until I felt sick as a dog. I had the worst headache in the world and my eyes were not the only thing watering; I could hardly bloody move. I spent the entire game on the bench completed zonked out, praying I wouldn't be called into action.

I got on the paddock for Otago for the first time when the team played Canterbury in Christchurch, but it was the following match, against South Canterbury in Timaru, that really sticks in my memory. I scored the best try of my life in that game. I went about 70 metres and beat half the team and got one under the posts. It was a dream scenario. And that was the start of it really. (If anyone's got that on film I'd love to have it for posterity.)

The nucleus of the Otago team was that Varsity A team — we were a bunch of Scarfies really. Everyone was so laidback. We'd all come from an amateur background of course, and most of us were free-spirited, fun-loving guys who just wanted to go out there and have fun. We were all great mates and the rugby, at both a club and provincial level, reflected that. The ethos of the team and the coaches meant we did some surprising things, even though we weren't the best team on paper. We didn't look like we had a chance of competing with the likes of Auckland, but we were encouraged to throw it around and have a bit of fun, and we played some of the most attractive rugby in the NPC, I think.

The Otago team was fantastic. Laurie was a superb coach. I really responded to his style of coaching. He was quite gruff and didn't care if he hurt your feelings. If he thought you had played like shit, he would let you know loud and clear. That was cool with me, because I like to know exactly where I stand.

I was surprised to read in Anton Oliver's book that he didn't get on with Laurie. I thought that the pair of them would get on like a house on fire because they are quite similar. They're both old school, very focused, and very, very professional. Then again, I was young, 19 years old, when I was coached by Laurie, so I didn't dare think of questioning him or his methods. It might have been different had I met him a few years on, after umpteen tests for the All Blacks, like Anton did.

We had some great personalities in the Otago team. Everyone had a nickname. Nicknames were all about finding a weakness, then sticking the knife in. Stu Forster was a midget, and shaped like a peg, so he was called The Poison Dwarf, Half-pint, Nipper, The Hook-Nosed Arab, Budgie Boy, and Festis. He was agile, though, and a tough little bugger and he could throw incredible one-arm passes. He was also the tightest man I ever met, hence his other nicknames like Gorse Pockets and Cobweb.

John Leslie tells a classic Forster story. He was coming home in a taxi one night when the taxi driver asked, 'You live with Stu Forster, don't you?'.

'Yeah, that's right,' JL said.

'He's the cheapest guy I've ever come across,' the taxi driver said and went on to say that Stu always tried to pay for his ride home with Otago kit — socks, ties, etc. JL realised that was where all *his* kit, which had been mysteriously disappearing from the flat, had got to.

JL was known as Chicken Shanks, Wheat Sacks and Lazy Eye. He was one of my best mates in the team. He was really serious about his rugby and he didn't like anything to break his routine, but he was one of the best dudes in the side and after the game he was a bundle of laughs. He would have been a brilliant All Black (especially given how well he played for Scotland), but his chance never came. It's a shame because he would have done the All Blacks proud and wouldn't have let anyone down.

JL used to get a bit of a bung eye when he was a bit tired or after a couple of beers. You'd look over at him and one eye would be going left and the other right. Johnny Timu suffered from it too, and Stu Forster and I would have bets on how many beers it would take for them to get the wandering retina.

Arran Pene was Calf-head or Hereford Head, and Dave Latta was Crazy. Anton was Hatchet Head and Grenade Face. Jeff Wilson was Golden Nuts and Hitler Youth. Jamie Joseph was Fly Back and Jake the Muss.

Stephen Bachop had plenty of names: Snake Handler (due to a very slippery mullet), Chubby Sten, Fat Sten, Obese Sten and Pumpkin (because he turned into a pumpkin after midnight). He got the name Chubby Sten when he, Stu, Josh Kronfeld, JL, Johnny Timu, myself and a few others went to the Apia Sevens with Gordy Hunter. One of the locals came up to us and proudly said, 'My favourite player is Stephen Bachop', but with his accent it sounded more like Sten Bach. Bach, who was plumper than most of us, became Chubby Sten from that moment on.

The Apia Sevens was some of the roughest footie I've ever seen. There'd be a real carnival feel, but the locals from the outlying areas who came in to watch bayed for blood. They'd sit in the stand under umbrellas, hopeful that a skinny white guy would get around a big local, so they could scream and laugh at him for being beaten.

The locals screamed even more when a big local guy took the head off a skinny white guy. There was a guy from an Auckland team at that tournament, Aaron Hamilton, who was really quick, a sort of sevens specialist before there was ever such a thing. He embarrassed a few locals on the field, but he would eventually get caught and dropped, and would have to be helped from the field. The crowd loved it. Being skinny and of Anglo-Saxon descent I was a real target too. I got my bell rung several times, majorly once, in a kamikaze tackle by a guy not much bigger than me. If he'd been any bigger I would have been in serious trouble.

Every year at the sevens, Cindy the local fa'afafine would make an appearance. Cindy was a local legend and quite clearly a bloke.

If you'd been to the sevens before (as I had, for Wellington, in 1990), you knew all about her, but after a few beers, she tended to fool the odd player there for the first time, especially once they'd had a few. It generally happened to the props and the locks, who had lower standards than anyone else: some poor uninformed guy would end up on the dance floor with Cindy, or worse, go in for a kiss, and we'd all be in hysterics.

Steve Hotton was one of the real characters of the Otago team. Every team has a guy like The Hot, who because of his personality is as valuable off the field as on. Hottie was my idol because he had his own fan club, the most impressive ginger moustache, and some good tattoos including a full back Pegasus. I've always been an admirer of a good 'tache. Tom Selleck, who I'd love to meet one day, ran a beauty. I've tried to emulate it a few times (and failed miserably). The founders of the Steve Hotton Fan Club, who apparently started the club just to get some university funding, came along to games wearing T-shirts with big moustaches on them.

For my initiation after my first game for Otago, Hottie and the others who ran the back seat (Dave Latta, Dick Knight and Gordy Macpherson, all tight forwards who had played more than 100 games for Otago) demanded I sit on the floor of the bus in front of the back seat, shut my eyes and face the front. They made me skull a beer, then gave me a biff in the head from behind. I had to guess who hit me each time: each wrong answer, another beer. Once I got it right three times, I was released. It took about eight cans. Futile bloody game, but I thought it was quite funny and it was a reminder of who the seniors and juniors were.

Because I was a skinny bastard they then made me climb above the seats into the area where the bags went. I had to wriggle along it until I was above the seat of Gerry Simmons, our manager (who was sitting up the front with Laurie) then flop one arm down and slap him across the head. He'd turn around and see nothing behind him, and couldn't work out how that was happening. It took a few slaps for Gerry to figure it out, much to the amusement of the fellas.

Hottie took me under his wing after that. He was a gnarled old prop and I was a sprightly 19-year-old winger, so we were an unlikely couple, but he had a beaut sense of humour and we became good mates. Over the years he gave me some fairly sound (and some bloody awful) advice.

Hottie was known as The White Pointer because he had a habit of pointing at players in the opposing team. It was a form of absolute intimidation: if you got the point you knew you were for it — Hottie was going to get you at the bottom of a ruck and, if you were unlucky, spread your nose across your face. At Carisbrook games he'd even point at the odd touch judge, who knew well enough that that meant he was to avert his gaze into the crowd while Hottie thumped somebody.

We trained at Tahuna Park, the most windswept, godforsaken ground in the world. You could literally see the southern front, which we affectionately called the Tahuna Doctor, coming in from Antarctica, and on a cold day half of the field would be frozen solid with ice. Nobody wanted to tackle because we'd cut ourselves on the ice, so we'd play on only half of the field. Laurie considered himself to be quite a hard fella in those days and pretty strong physically as well. At training he worked the forwards into the ground, hitting tackle bags until their ears were bleeding and they were foaming at the mouth. Gordy, as assistant coach, would be standing on the back of the bags eyeballing the players as they hit the ruck and Laurie would be standing alongside, thumping the bags, yelling, 'Take it here fellas, in here'. One day, during a particularly tough training, Hottie had had enough. He broke loose of the pack, came sweeping around from Laurie's blind spot, and drove him into the base of the tackle bags. The forward pack went straight over the top of him, boots flying. When Laurie got up he was bleeding and his hair was all over the place.

'Fellas, that will be the end of training. I know you're there mentally,' Laurie said, and limped off. Hottie was stoked with himself. It was one of the funniest things I have seen.

I used to give Hottie a bit of friendly shit. One day, in a club game, we were thumping Southern by an astronomical amount. I must have been giving Hottie a hard time because he gave me the point during the game. 'Oh Jesus, I am really for it now,' I thought.

Within five minutes I found myself trapped at the bottom of a ruck with my hands pinned at the side, just my head and shoulders hanging out. I saw Hottie's eyes light up as he came running in from about 10 metres. I shut my eyes, thinking 'Oh God, here it comes'. And when I opened them Hottie was giving me a kiss on the cheek.

Sometimes I got a slap around the chops. One day I was being a cheeky sod to Arran Pene. In those days Arran was the father figure of the team. During this particular training he was a little on edge. He had been injured for the previous couple of games and replaced by Taine Randell who had played bloody well. A few of us wound him up, saying we had overheard Gordy saying that Arran was on the way out.

In the warm-up drills I threw a few balls at Arran's feet. 'Shit mate, switch on sausage fingers,' I'd call out and Gordy would turn around and see Arran fumbling away with the ball. The shit-stirring continued and in the final warm-up drill, one where we rolled the ball from one player to another, Arran positioned himself opposite me. When I rolled the ball to him he scooped it up with his left hand and gave me a straight right.

I didn't wake up until the boys were doing their stretches at the end of the drill. It was probably a powder-puff hit by Calf Head's standards, but it was the last thing I needed on the Thursday before a game against Canterbury. I had earned it, though, and Arran's a man of his word — he had been promising to knock me out for a long time.

Southern TV were there for the training run and they caught the whole thing on film. On it you can see that once his right hand connected with my chin, Arran's smile went from ear to ear.

JL and I used to have a shower together after training and spin a bit of shit. One day, Anton Oliver, who at the tender age of 18 had just had his first training with the Otago team, sauntered into the showers. Anton is a big, raw-boned character, and is built like that from top to toe. Naturally JL and I couldn't help but comment. We wholeheartedly congratulated him on his major point of difference. Poor Anton freaked and was showered, dried and driving home within two minutes.

In the court session after that Saturday's game I was one of the two judges. We asked that everyone bring their gold coins up to the bench. Everyone obliged and I put about $50 in coins in a neat line along the front of the bench. We then asked Anton to come up the front and 'present arms' so to speak, and measure up against the gold coins. To cut a long story short it was a get-rich-quick scheme for Anton, who got to keep all the coins (and could have kept the desk as well if he'd wanted).

* * *

The play back then was pretty rough and tumble. My job as a wing was to finish the moves, collect box kicks, and place the ball for the forwards to drive over. In my early days in the team Mike Brewer would kick me in the guts or stand on me as he went over the top of me at training. At first I thought he was un-co, or a bit of a wanker, but he was neither. It was just his way of hardening me up for the real thing. I had to earn my stripes. ('Bruiser' used to tell a funny story of his first meeting with my hero Murray Mexted. It was in Wellington, under the stand at Athletic Park, where team captains went for the coin toss before the start of a match. Murray was the incumbent All Blacks number eight, and Mike was a well-known number eight too. Bruiser offered his hand to Murray, saying, 'Gidday, Mike Brewer'. Mex replied, 'Sorry, Mike who?'.)

What was acceptable play then is quite different to what's legal now. You really could use your feet in those days. Rucking was encouraged, but we were told never to ruck anyone by ourselves, the philosophy being that if two guys are rucking somebody they can't both be sent off. Laurie and Gordy also used to say, 'Go for the bony parts' — the boys would be hoeing into people's knees, elbows and ankles because they could do a lot more damage there than on thighs or calves. I used to love watching them from the back as they really got stuck into anyone who was on the wrong side of the ruck.

It wasn't so much fun being on the receiving end. I was lucky that Hottie and a few of the bigger guys looked out for me most of the time. When I went to the bottom of a ruck they would flop on top of me and get booted instead of me. I could feel the hits through their bodies, but then they'd get up and give me a bit of a wink. It was an extraordinarily tight team in that way.

I got caught on the wrong side of an Auckland ruck once at Carisbrook and they really dealt to me. Forwards, particularly guys like Fitzy and the Brooke brothers, loved to catch backs on the wrong side, and they would actually laugh while they were having a go. Taking it on the chin was a source of pride for the Otago boys, so I told myself to keep quiet and not make any noise (a damn sight easier said than done). I got up as fast as I could afterwards and ran off as if nothing had happened. Shit, it hurt though . . .

In my third match for Otago, against Canterbury, I replaced John Timu, who was away at the World Cup, and I got two tries. By then we had a good chance of winning the NPC, so long as we won the next four games in a row.

We went on to beat Auckland down in Dunedin. I was marking Eroni Clarke on the wing. He was about 105 kilos, so he was a giant compared to me, but I managed to have a pretty good game. It wasn't a full-strength Auckland side, because the All Blacks were away, but so too were a couple of Otago's key players. That was a key win for us as we were just a couple of wins away from taking our first National Provincial Championship title.

In the final match of the season we faced North Harbour at Carisbrook. I got a try in the corner at one stage and we went on to win the match. It was a splendid feeling to be a part of an NPC-winning side in my first year in Dunedin. I almost couldn't believe it!

The celebration that night was a beauty. The team had dinner at Larnach Castle. We were all allowed to invite a partner and I knew just who I wanted to take as there was a girl in my hostel who I had a bit of a soft spot for. Sadly, I didn't get the chance to invite her. One of our props, Steve Cumberland, asked me if I had a girlfriend. When I said no, he said, 'Great, you're taking Cheryl to the dinner'. Even though I had no idea who Cheryl was, I was not about to argue with Cumby.

That night I collected Cheryl from South Dunedin in a cab (which was very expensive for a student with very little money) and took the corsage Cumby had ordered me to buy to 'make her feel special'. I was 19 and Cheryl was pushing 30 (and showing signs of wear and tear) so Cumby's threat of 'no silly business' was a moot point. It turned out

Cumby wanted her there just in case: 'I needed a back-up, in case the bird I took didn't put out,' he told me.

Carisbrook is my favourite rugby ground in the world. In those days 20,000 or so people would turn up at the House of Pain for a big game. Perhaps because of the varsity feel to the team, all the students used to come along and the terraces were a beaut, fun place to be. Bottles of beer were still allowed, so everyone would have a couple of beers and get into it. People would drag couches in to sit on, and every now and then set them on fire.

As we ran onto the field we'd be confronted by a sea of blue and gold in the stands. The crowd would go nuts. You just can't help but play well in that environment. You're lifted by the crowd. And when you score a try in front of a crowd like that, you get the most amazing adrenalin rush you could ever get. It's a feeling that is very hard to articulate.

Whenever we had a home game Laurie took the team to a hotel in Mosgiel the night before. Once we got there we would sit down and have a team meeting. Laurie would pull out his notebook and slowly look around the room, giving every player the stare. Occasionally, his gaze would rest on someone in particular and he'd proceed to give them a rocket. It was quite a horrific experience sitting there waiting to see who he'd pick on and I never knew how to take it. It was pure psychology, I guess.

Gordy was the opposite. He was the guy who would come up to you and quietly say, 'I need two tries out of you today, lad'. He would always, always sit down with me before a game and have a whisper in my ear. It might only be a couple of sentences, but it really meant something. It really mattered that he did that.

The night before the critical final match of the 1991 NPC against North Harbour, I was rooming with Arthur Stone. Arthur had the double bed (in the Otago team, just like in the All Blacks, the senior players get the double bed and the more junior roommate is relegated to the single). I was looking forward to more sleep than I'd get on a Friday night at Unicol, but Arthur liked to go out for a few beers to ensure a good sleep. He came in at about midnight, thumped around for a while, turned on the TV and promptly fell asleep, happily snoring away with the TV hissing in the background and the lights on.

The day of a game we would all meet for breakfast at 10 a.m., and then the backs would get together and spend an hour or so going through their moves. For a 2 p.m. kick-off we'd all be on the bus in our Number Ones by 12.30 p.m. We all sat in the same seat each week. I sat behind Arran Pene, so I used to get a bit bus-sick: his neck and head were so big I couldn't see out of the front of the bus.

There would be absolute silence on the bus. Nobody talked at all. Everyone kept to themselves. Some people have certain habits and rituals, things that they are superstitious about. It's all personal. I liked to have the same routine before every single game. At midday I always polished my boots. I wore the same pair of togs under my rugby shorts every time I played and before running out of the changing room onto the field I did 20 press-ups and 20 sit-ups.

After every game we couldn't wait to get into the changing rooms for the court session. It was a controlled opportunity to let your hair down with just the team. Each session started with admin, a little word from manager Gerry Simmons. There were always a couple of judges who ran the court. They announced the rules each week. The rules were very strict and I loved the discipline they required and the respect that was shown for everyone in the team, regardless of how long you'd been in it.

The judges would appoint 'pimps', three or four whose job it was to dob in anyone who spoke out of turn or broke the rules. This was an esteemed position and if they dobbed you in, you were punished.

There'd usually be a team comment: everyone got to finish their beer, stand up, and make a comment, usually just half a dozen words to explain what the game, or the day, had meant to them. Everyone got a chance to have a say and we were judged on what we said, not who we were.

The court would be opened up for fines. Members of the team could raise an accusation (often fabricated) about another team member. It was usually best not to defend an accusation. There would be mandatory joke-telling from a few nominated players, and you certainly didn't want to be caught telling a dud.

There was lots of drinking and some silly behaviour in those court sessions — which I always applauded. Much has been said of the asinine nature of the drinking culture of rugby teams. For what it's worth, I think it was a vital ingredient in the success of the Otago team of the early 1990s. The game was amateur and to savour the moment with a beer or three with your team-mates was the reward at the end of a match. The court session was about discipline and respect and seldom did we overstep the mark and become anti-social. When we did, we would be pulled back into line. The same could not always be said of the University club, but standards of behaviour within the confines of a university environment tend to be more liberal.

The court sessions for Varsity A really could run amuck. I learnt quickly that I should do my best to keep my head down and obey the rules. Talking out of turn was forbidden and if you were caught you had to go up the front and have a jug. Justin Cullen was always caught. JC was another of the real characters of club rugby in Dunedin (he's playing club rugby for Varsity now, more than a decade on, in Wellington). He had a booming voice and could never resist trying to have a whisper to his neighbour, so he was always getting picked on. He's an ox of a man, so skulling a jug wasn't the end of the world to him and didn't seem to work as a deterrent. The judges found the only way to keep him quiet was to get him to hold his old fella against the wall of the changing room. He used to sit, as luck would have it, in the southern corner of the changing room, the coldest corner because the wind hit the southern wall, so by the time he'd spent five minutes pressing his old fella against the concrete, he'd turn blue and we wouldn't get a bloody peep out of him for the rest of the court session.

We did nude 400-metre runs, where the last one back was locked outside. The varsity clubrooms would be full of people and the team would come tearing out naked and sprint around the field.

One night, after being named a member of the All Blacks, John Timu jumped into his VW and celebrated with some paddock work on the grounds. Rex Thompson, the president of the club, came dashing out, swearing that whoever was driving would never play for University again. He changed his mind when JT jumped out.

The yellow tour-leader's jersey made a regular appearance at Varsity and Otago court sessions and was hotly contested in our drinking games. It was a yellow jersey, any yellow jersey that anyone brought along to a team drink, which was won and lost among the team. Whether the challenge was over a can or a jug of beer, the first to get to the bottom got the yellow jersey. It was an inane game, but one that was a huge amount of fun and it was all about tactics. If you waited till late in the night, when some of the guys started to get a little worse for wear, the chances of winning the jersey were higher.

We were always on the hunt for the best tour-leader's jersey. After an Otago game one night, I went into McDonald's at about 2 a.m. and spied a guy of about 18, from an Otago track and field team, in a yellow adidas three-stripe tracksuit. It was the full kit, with the stirrup pants and everything, and I offered him my Otago tie for the tracksuit, which he agreed to. He stripped off and gave it to me (and then security threw him out for being naked). For the next few years that zip-up jacket was the tour-leader's jersey. Somebody would turn up to a court session with it every now and then and we'd have a massive session vying for it.

One particular evening Dave Latta and I were the last men standing after a fairly hefty court session. I won the yellow jersey off him and sprinted off, hoping to avoid a rematch. Mandy was in Dunedin hospital recovering from a back operation, so I headed off to the hospital and got buzzed in after-hours under the guise of paying her a visit. I figured Dave would never follow me into the hospital, so I was safe and sound, but his wife Tracey was a nurse so he got in under the ruse of coming to visit her and chased me all around the hospital with two cans of beer in his pocket, wanting to win back the jersey. Fortunately, I lost him and I rubbed it in the next day by charging into the team photo at Carisbrook on a mate's Vespa, wearing the yellow jersey, punching the air with one fist. (For the record, I was late as usual and missed the photo altogether.)

Half a Pound of Cat's Meat

Winning the NPC was a great end to 1991. So was the Varsity A crate day, an infamous end-of-season tradition. It was like a progressive dinner: a big bottle of beer was drunk at a team member's house, then you moved on to the next one, until you'd been to all twelve. The day was beautifully organised, so that things would happen along the way.

Your seniority in the team dictated how early or late your house would be visited. The first houses we visited were the homes of the old soldiers in the team. We'd sit around and drink out of glasses and nothing untoward would happen. By the fourth house, people would be getting a bit happy. By the sixth, which was always John Timu and Arran Pene's flat, 707 Cumberland Street, we'd all get nude and, as tradition dictated, 'dip our balls in the Leith'. We'd strip off, sprint across Cumberland Street, through the middle of varsity, and climb down the ladder opposite the university clock tower, into the water. It was freezing cold — you almost had to break a hole in the ice to get into the river — so no one looked his best on the way home, but it was a mandatory event and filled with much hilarity.

Houses eight to 12 always belonged to the lowliest in the team, because by the time the guys had had that many bottles of beer, the nonsense would start. My flat was number 12 one year and it didn't look good when at number 10, Tony Fordray's flat, the behaviour really started deteriorating. The mob mentality kicked in — once someone started trashing things, everyone jumped on the bandwagon, and the boys went through Tony's house like a dose of salts. One guy kicked down a fence, about 50 pickets. Someone else took out every window in the house. Another threw the TV into a brick wall outside. JL swung around and around the clothesline until it snapped. The climax was seeing Arran Pene on the roof wrestling the chimney off. It was moronic, but also highly amusing.

The police arrived once we started knocking over letterboxes on the street leading to the 11th house. Everyone was so sauced they didn't even try to run away. We all got caught and had to spend the money we'd chipped in for an end-of-year trip to Queenstown on fixing all the letterboxes, which we all conceded was fair.

The next stop, the 11th house, was a fairly sombre affair, given that the police had just told us off, but by the time the team got to my flat it all went absolutely pear-shaped. Our prop, Nick Moore, found a bike helmet, strapped it on and ran straight through the kitchen wall. Unfortunately, he hit the hot-water cylinder on the other side of the wall and knocked himself unconscious. As he fell he cut himself on the beer bottle he was clinging to, so we called an ambulance and had him removed.

Two minutes later someone got hit in the head with a full tin of baked beans and we had to call 111 again. The ambulance refused to come, which was fair enough, considering they'd been there five minutes ago and not been impressed with the state we were in, so we had to take the patient to the hospital in a cab. By the time I got home from the hospital Arran had emptied a beanbag in one room (which took days and days to vacuum up), and the contents of the pantry — Sunlight soap flakes, tins of food — had been thrown all around the house. It was an absolute disaster zone. It looked like someone had set off a bomb in the place. The next morning my three female flatmates were suitably unimpressed.

A couple of days later Jock Hobbs came to stay and my flatmates decided it was time to pay me back for the crate-day carnage.

Jock Hobbs: I went down to Dunedin to watch the Otago University club sides. Everything was done on a shoestring with New Zealand Universities, so I stayed at Marc's flat. It was freezing cold, Spartan, and there was nothing to eat. You had to have the fire going all the time to get any warmth. He had kindly given me his bed, but when I got into it, it had been sandbagged. It was full of beanbag beans.

It had been the most extraordinary 12 months of my life so far. It was my first year out of school. I'd moved to Dunedin and gone into a NPC-winning Otago side and a side, more importantly, full of such good buggers.

I ended up having 70-odd games for Otago in the following years and I never would have got that first big break if John Timu hadn't gone away with the All Blacks. If I had to go back and choose only one team to ever play for, I'm not sure it would be the All Blacks. It would probably be Otago. I was very lucky to be around during what turned out to be a unique time in Otago rugby.

* * *

In 1992 Laurie was made the All Blacks coach and Gordy Hunter became the Otago coach. I knew my second year in the team would be the hardest — people were on their guard waiting to see how I'd do and John Timu was back with the Otago team, so I decided to pick a position and try to make it my own. I went for centre and managed to break my way in before too long.

It was the amateur days, so we only trained on Tuesdays and Thursdays, but on those days Gordy used to train us like dogs. Tuesday training involved serious fitness: sprints from one dead-ball line to another called 150s; 60 or so tackle bags; and endless 'down and ups'. Afterwards I'd be shattered. Thursday was team drills, which were exhausting too, but I used to enjoy watching Gordy make the forwards scrum and scrum and scrum, while he lay under the scrum machine, an inch away from their faces, staring at them or screaming 'Push!'.

Gordy was one of the world's greatest guys. He wasn't the greatest coach in the world — as an ex-wing he had limitations in terms of guiding the forwards of the team in certain intricacies — but he was the best manager of men I have ever come across. As a motivator, a guy who could instil a feeling of loyalty and passion just by the way he did things, he was second to none. Gordy cared about honesty, integrity and trust, and he cultivated those qualities in his players. When we went out onto the field and played against the likes of Auckland (which had 13 All Blacks then) we never gave up. We played for each other. There was implicit trust among all of us. No matter what position you found yourself in, on or off the field, you knew you'd be backed up.

We called Gordy The Riddler because he was hugely eccentric and he had an amazing way with words. If he wanted to screw with your mind, by God he would. He was also really funny. He used to do a rendition of 'Eenie Meenie Minie Mo' that was hilarious and included the line 'half a pound of cat's meat'. Once, in the middle of a performance of it, he got so excited he booted a chair, which flew across the room, and straight into the face of Stan To'omalatai. Stan, who is a bloody big guy, just sat there and took it on the chin. Years later he named his son Carisbrook Gordon.

Gordy very rarely talked about how he lost his eye, but about once a year, when he needed to, he'd pull out what we called the 'They Stole My Eye' speech. We'd be sitting in the team room the night before the game, and he'd start. For many of the new guys, it would be the first time they'd heard Gordy speak about his eye. They'd sit bolt upright and start looking very nervous.

Gordy had a deep voice that would break when he became emotional and he would go on and on about 'they' and how they'd stolen his eye and how he'd managed to achieve the goals he'd set himself in spite of them. It was all about overcoming adversity and he'd tell it for a reason, to get us ready for the next day's game but, to this day, I have no idea who 'they' were, because Gordy went blind in a workshop accident when a splinter flew into his eye.

I hope for their sake 'they' never got caught by Gordy. A policeman first and foremost, he was a harder breed of copper than we know now. In the court sessions he would entertain us with his 'Hunter Files', stories about his police work. Judging by them he had some fairly unorthodox techniques that had criminals confessing to all sorts of things. He was the last guy I would ever have wanted interrogating me.

One night on the plonk with the team in Napier, we ended up at the Masonic pub. Half a dozen of us had outstayed most of the locals and we came up with the ingenious idea of bar dives. We took turns jumping off the bar while the others stood below with their arms out, but when Arran dove off the bar nobody was there to catch him and he went straight through a table. Crazy Dave Latta and I ran through a false wall.

Early the next morning word got back to Gordy that our behaviour had been less than ideal. He got us out of bed at 7 a.m. (most of us had got home only three hours before) and sent us on a blow-out for two hours. Towards the end he made us all run into a crash pad he was holding, over and over again. Nick Moore, our prop, tripped as he ran into the pad and fell on Gordy's knee, but Gordy carried on with training. Two weeks later Gordy came to training with a brace on. When quizzed he explained that he had ruptured his knee ligaments when Nick fell on him and he'd had to have an operation to fix it. Most people would have to be helped from the field with such an injury, but Gordy kept on punishing us that day and never said a word about his leg until he had to.

In 2000, Gordy came north to coach Auckland and he and his wife Jenny lived in my house in Remuera, while I went flatting. They looked after my cat and I loved being able to pop in for a cuppa with them. Then, while Gordy was still with Auckland, I went south to play for Otago again and it was strange to be in the Otago team and play against Gordy's Auckland side.

At JL's wedding, by which time Gordy was suffering from cancer, our great friend made a speech. A lot of our mates, the ones who didn't play rugby, had heard about how good a Gordy Hunter speech was, but that day they were treated to a beauty. Gordy stood up and spoke about how, around the time of picking JL as the captain of Otago, he was visited by God, who told him to pick the one with the skinny legs. It was a mesmerising speech, what with his trademark mannerisms and his pregnant pauses.

After he died the Gordon Hunter Memorial Trophy was created, and every time Auckland plays Otago for it, it is a very special day for all of us who played under Gordy. He and Jenny were just wonderful people and cool mates. He was a beautiful man.

When the Varsity A club side was announced in 1992, a few of the boys and I went out for some celebratory beers. On the way back home through Scarfieville the call came out to start throwing around the rubbish bins on the footpath, out for collection the next day, and we gleefully left a trail of destruction behind us, knowing that some of our mates were on the Saturday morning clean-up crew of students on probation sent out to clean the streets.

When we got to the campus Commerce building we spied a crane. Tony Hunt, Waffle and I climbed up, even though there were signs saying not to, 10 storeys or so. We sat there admiring the view for a while, feeling fairly pleased with ourselves.

Out of the corner of my eye I noticed a dog, a big Alsatian, on the road. I thought it had been run over, but then I spied another. The dogs were followed by the Boys in Blue, which got the three of us very excited. Maybe they were about to apprehend a robber. We'd be able to watch the whole thing unfold from our lookout. Then, through a loudhailer, we heard, 'Get down from the crane'. The police were after us!

We decided it would be a good idea to resist arrest at that stage, so politely suggested that the police come up and get us. This poor cop started climbing up, stopping to yell, 'Come down', every now and then (only to hear, 'No, come and get us', in reply). When he finally reached us, I realised we were being pursued by our mate Hunter Darry. Hunter was a regular in the Otago B team at that stage, but also played a number of games for Otago. He was a great mate of Gordy's and I knew I was about to be in big trouble when Gordy got wind of this. I had nothing to lose, or so I thought, so I told Hunter I was going to climb down and try to outrun the police dogs. I asked Hunter to say he didn't know who I was if I managed to get away. It was a stupid idea — one of the dogs was the number-two attack dog in New Zealand and would have had me in seconds — and eventually Hunter convinced me to come down quietly. He then made us pick up every piece of litter bigger than a 20-cent piece strewn around the neighbourhood. It was a fitting punishment, and better than having to face Gordy.

Otago had another cracker NPC season in 1992 and in the final we faced Waikato up in Hamilton. That whole trip was quite a wild affair. We hated playing Waikato because they were always a bloody hard side to beat, particularly if we were playing them at home. They had fantastic fans. These guys would turn up outside our hotel room at 3 a.m., clanging cowbells and trying to keep us Otago players up through the night (which they did a fairly effective job of). The day of a game it would look like all of Hamilton had come out to support their team — they would line the main road ringing bells, and have floats and all sorts of things.

The Otago team went up there a couple of nights before the game. A few of the boys went out for a beer on the Thursday. Later on in the night John Timu happened to be dancing beside some random girl on the dance floor. It was absolutely low-key, nothing in it, but her boyfriend wasn't happy. He came out of nowhere, king-hit JT, and knocked him out. We all woke up on the Friday morning to the news that our best player was ruled out of the NPC final because he had been dropped by some Hamilton bogan's cheap shot. (Gordy apparently made sure the guy got the book thrown at him by the local police.)

The dirty tricks continued at the game that Saturday. Just a few minutes into it Richard Loe (who is actually a bloody beaut bloke) tried to hook Greg Cooper's eye out of his head. He didn't even try to hide it in the ruck; he just lent over and tried to scoop one of Cooper's digits out of his helmet.

Gordy used to say, 'They can't play with one eye', but that was one of the most blatant examples of thuggery I have ever seen in rugby. The Otago team naturally got up in arms about it, and we got a hiding in that game.

* * *

Once I'd made the Otago team for the second year, I decided that if I outplayed every opponent I marked, I might have a chance of getting in the All Blacks. Laurie had only coached me for six games the year before, but I had gone alright in those games. I thought that would have to count for something.

Sure enough I got called up for the All Blacks trial in Napier. I was ecstatic to be included — to get an All Blacks trial was a huge honour — and it felt like a continuation of the dream run. The trials went alright. I got a try, but then missed John Kirwan in a bloody awful tackle, which allowed him to score. In spite of that I was named in the '92 All Blacks squad.

Laurie Mains: What he displayed led me to believe he could be an All Black. He got it a little sooner than he or I might have expected, but because of how he played for Otago he was in my mind.

Anne Ellis: We were standing with him in Napier when they announced the team. Chris and I had driven up from Wellington and when Marc's name was announced I looked over at Marc, and there was this huge smile. I'll always remember that. And that Mike Brewer was the first over to congratulate him.

It was a pretty momentous occasion, really exciting, and the first thing that crossed my mind was that now that I had been named an All Black, I had to become a good one. It was even more special because it was the centenary of the New Zealand Rugby Union that year and I travelled to Christchurch as part of the centenary tour. A World XV had been put together to play the All Blacks and I hoped to get a game against them, but that didn't eventuate. I guess the All Blacks wanted to win all of the games, so they put Frank Bunce at centre and John Kirwan and Inga Tuigamala on the wings. Perhaps because of my size I didn't have the full confidence of the coaches in my ability to assert the physical presence they wanted. The All Blacks mentality at the time was to have big centres that hit the ball up and then turned over second-phase ball to the forwards to recycle. I wasn't big enough to be overly confrontational, but if the opportunity was there to have a go on the outside I invariably would.

I watched the three centenary tests as a non-playing reserve on the sideline, but did make it onto the field once, before the first test, to receive my centenary cap. The Otago players were received pretty well, but when the Auckland players came out to collect their caps a few of them got boos, which showed the parochial nature of Christchurch.

My roommate on that trip to Christchurch — my first roommate ever in the All Blacks — was John Kirwan. JK was one of my heroes, just the coolest guy as far as I was concerned, and in person he was just a nice, laidback guy (not at all big-headed like you might think a guy like him might have been in his prime). The protocol, just as in the Otago team, was that the junior All Blacks got the single bed in the hotel rooms; the senior players the double. JK said we'd toss a coin for the bed, which I thought was pretty cool: the greatest winger ever in All Blacks history and he tossed a coin for the double bed. That humility showed me that he was a top guy.

JK has a nice calmness about him. At that stage he was working on the mental side of the game. Physically, he had done everything he could possibly do to improve himself, so he was developing his mental focus. He did exercises: he used to visualise what he would do when he got the ball, and in quiet moments he would pull out a piece of string with a rugby stud tied onto it and sit there holding it, trying to get it moving in certain directions with his mind.

The thing that defines the great players I have met is their mental state, their self-belief, and their desire to make a difference. In top-level sport it's all about mental fitness. A lot of it is a confidence thing: it's about playing care-free and having the confidence to have a crack. When your tail is up, when you believe you are going to be the one that scores the winning try, you play well. When your tail's down and you don't want to be the guy who drops the ball or misses a losing tackle, you don't always play so well.

The coach has a big part to play in that. He has to fill you with confidence, with the desire to have a go and not to worry about making a mistake. If he creates an environment bred of fear, as opposed to one that is founded on the excitement of success, then you can find yourself hamstrung. One of Laurie's great calls was 'Dump it and move on'. He knew that to get us to play at the top level there had to be room to play risky rugby, rugby where a player might make a mistake, but would also be more likely to do something brilliant. If we made a mistake we were to forget about it. It's a good philosophy to apply to anything in life, I think. If you make a mistake, dump it and move on. If you do something good, do the same. There is no point in dwelling on the past, either way.

I am so lucky to have played both amateur and professional rugby because there is such a disparity between the two. Back in the amateur days we were doing it for all the right reasons: we were proud of representing our region or our country and we really wanted to give our utmost. We had such a positive culture behind us, from the coaches down to the public who supported us. At the beginning of the year, Gordy Hunter would say, 'You are my centre for the season'. That meant you could be secure in that position, know that whatever you did, you still had your place. We weren't inhibited by the fear of making a mistake.

In the modern professional game there is such pressure on players. If they make a mistake it's not just a blow to the team and the club, and their supporters; the player can theoretically lose his contract. If he has a couple of bad games there is a chance that he is going to get moved on. That creates an environment where you can't really feel free and uninhibited and you become more concerned with your individual performance than the team result.

After the centenary celebrations the All Blacks went on tour to Australia and South Africa. It was a fantastic tour. We had a bloody good team and management. We had a few guys from Otago in there, including Arran Pene, Jamie Joseph and Johnny Timu. Ric Salizzo was the media liaison officer (which basically meant he had to keep Laurie away from the media, with whom he had a real love/hate relationship).

Ric Salizzo, creator and co-host of 'Sports Café': I used to sit on the bus next to Sean Fitzpatrick. The captain and management had to sit up the front, and so did the new boys, so Macca and Matt Cooper sat behind us. Every day Macca took the piss out of Matt Cooper. Fitzy and I would be in hysterics listening to him. Matt's the nicest guy in the world, so he'd say something and Macca would just rip him apart. It was very funny. That was my first introduction to Marc.

There was a hierarchy in the touring side. I understood that the older boys were down the back of the bus and I had to sit up the front. It was a matter of biding my time and keeping my head low to earn my stripes. The hierarchy in the team was important. The senior players had learnt team traditions from the senior players before them and that created the ethos of the team. They passed them down to the young ones and everyone was respectful of the All Black traditions and the players who had come before. The older players were good at sharing their knowledge about what we were trying to achieve and the various protocols, and ensured that the young guys didn't put a foot wrong. That kept us on the straight and narrow, I reckon, and the link to the All Blacks of the past was kept because of those traditions.

On tour there are always committees, and at the beginning of the Australian tour I was put in charge of organising music for a one-off team party. That was the only time I got asked to do that: I got a very, very bad band along (I don't know what they were called, but they played the sort of music I was into at the time) and it didn't really light the candle of some of the older boys. After that I was told to focus on my laundry duties with Matt Cooper.

Laundry is the one committee you didn't want to get; it's a prick of a job. After training the guys went into their rooms, stripped off, and threw their laundry out into the corridor. Matt and I had to go around and pick up everyone's bloody laundry and put it into bags to be sent off to be washed. When the laundry came back all clean we had to go through it and sort out whose was whose. I hated doing that, so I would intentionally mix everyone's stuff up in the vain hope the players would complain and I would get moved onto another committee.

News of Richard Loe's eye-gouging attack in the NPC final had travelled around the world and arrived in Australia before us. Everyone was calling Loey a thug, and he lived up to his reputation when, in one of the tests against Australia, Paul Carozza dived over in the corner to score a try. Loey, who was coming across in cover defence, but didn't make it in time, came in on top of him and gave him a forearm right on the nose. He smashed Paul's nose all over his face. It was horribly late (but I have to admit that sitting in the grandstand I gave a little squeal of delight) and Loey was suspended for a couple of games.

I got my first All Blacks game against a South Australian Invitational team in Adelaide. That game should have been the highlight of my rugby career so far, but I went on the field with mixed feelings. Just a day or two before the game I got word that my friend Sam Williams had died in a snowboarding accident in Queenstown. In those days the news of the day came through to the team via faxes circulated on the bus each morning. Sam's death had made the papers and as I read about it on the bus I couldn't believe it; I had to read the story over and over again before it sank in. Sam was a great snowboarder, but while boarding in Queenstown he had hit a bit of tussock and landed on his neck. He was taken to the spinal unit in Christchurch and put on life support, but a couple of days later he made the decision to turn the machines off. How incredibly brave. Apparently, when he passed away, he gave his folks a big grin, and that's the way I remember Sam to this day, with a smile on his face.

I was torn between playing my first game for the All Blacks and going back to New Zealand to attend the funeral of my close friend. The All Blacks management were great, really supportive, and in the end I decided that Sam would want me to hang around and play the game and do my best for him, so that was what I did but, to be honest, my first game for the All Blacks didn't mean a hell of a lot to me. I felt as though I shouldn't have been there. I should have been in Gisborne, with all of my friends, at my mate's funeral.

The tour continued and we went up to the top of Australia, by the Great Barrier Reef, for a mid-week game. I was rooming with Kevin Schuler. We got on bloody well — Herb could make me laugh and laugh. He was a great fan of hotel bathrobes. He would arrive at a hotel, get into the room, and immediately stick on the robe. I took to that with great gusto too and the pair of us would stride around the hotel in our robes, thinking we looked like Hugh Hefner. We'd never get to sleep at night because we'd be saying and doing stupid things to crack each other up. The Jerky Boys were a comedy duo who were big at the time. They would make classic threatening crank calls to randoms to freak them out. Just as I would be going off to sleep, Herb would yell out one or other of their lines and we would erupt in giggles.

The team was taken out on a boat for a snorkel around the reef one afternoon and it wasn't long before Michael Jones was recognised by a couple of Japanese tourists on the boat, who had their photo taken with him and bought him an ice cream. Michael, being such a lovely chap, worried that he didn't know how to say thank you in Japanese. I assured him that I was fluent in basic Japanese, and told him to go over, bow and nod, always keeping eye contact, while chanting 'Ditty mau, ditty mau'. Of course, I'd made the whole thing up (and was hoping like hell that it translated to something obscene), but Michael believed me and took off to find his fans. Herb and I crept down the back of the boat and watched as Michael was bowing and scraping before these poor girls, who stood there looking very confused and, after a while, a little bit scared. When Michael spied Herb and me cracking up he chased me around the boat. I spent 90 minutes hiding in the engine room as we made our way back to dock.

Nudity and beer . . . what a marriage.

My first year at Unicol. If you got too 'sideways' you lost your eyebrows, as Chesney (centre) found out.

Chesney and me warming up for our floor skit.

Unicol Yearbook, 1991

Our skit won! We shaved our heads on stage and then did a ballet routine entitled 'The Enchantment of the Bollock'.

Ellis Collection

The Murdoch-Ellis arm wrestling competition has been going since our first year at varsity, 1991.

Toby doing a 'yard' at one of our mate's Mexican-themed 21st party. I'm nervous as the next in line.

In no particular order . . .'Worzel Gummidge', 'Bert and Ernie', 'Frankenstein' and 'One Big Bitch'.

My flatmate Sniff trashing our Gore Place lounge.

Murray and Smiddy doing sick things with each other.

A JL party on the night of the infamous 'Fonzie Incident'. Peter looks to have spilt his cup of tea.

Counting the winnings after icing a Melbourne Cup trifecta. Higgsy, in the tartan shirt, later went to hospital to have splinters removed from his groin.

With the fence that Higgsy demolished, we started a fire. The fireman's face says it all. Great moustache!

The boys with the new flat vehicle, bought from Turner's. Riding on the back was always the favoured option.

Enjoying a fall of snow with flatmates Waffle and Linseo.

You need some serious protection from mosquitoes if you sleep under the stars on the West Coast.

Never were cars more important than at university. They were a sign to show you'd made it!

Fresh West Coast whitebait on a road-trip home to Wellington.

Princesses and Prize-fighters

Our next stop was South Africa. It was a difficult decision to make, whether I'd go on that tour or not. It was my first as an All Black, but I had protested against the Springbok tour to New Zealand in 1981 with my dad. I was taught, and I still believe, that there is a relationship between sport and politics and that by protesting it was made clear that New Zealand didn't support what was happening in South Africa. I am sure that will make me unpopular with some, but that's me and if we were all the same, life would be pretty boring.

Apartheid wasn't quite over in South Africa in 1992, but supposedly a new South Africa was in the making and in the end I decided to go and see for myself.

We arrived in Johannesburg at about 3 a.m. on a July morning. I was astounded to see hundreds of people waiting at the airport to welcome us. I hadn't realised the fanaticism of rugby fans in South Africa. It was an extraordinary scene; like we were rock stars or something and I have never seen anything like it since. Two weeks later the Aussie team, the current world champions, turned up at the same airport in the middle of the day and there were only 20 people there to greet them. I guess that illustrates the history and respect between New Zealand and South Africa when it comes to rugby.

Naturally, the South African Rugby Union wanted to turn it on for the All Blacks to make sure we saw how much South Africa had changed. As part of the attempt to show us the new South Africa the team was taken on a tour through Soweto. Our tour guide, a white South African, who I assumed had been hired by the South African Rugby Union, stood at the front of the bus and explained how Soweto had been transformed: schools were being set up and the whole slum was being tidied up. Then he went on to tell us that blacks were not human, not of the same 'species' as whites because their skulls were smooth like billiard balls, as opposed to the fractured cranium of the Anglo-Saxon. He had no qualms about voicing this nonsense to us (and seemed oblivious to the Maori and Pacific Island guys in the team) and he wasn't the only one to offer that view over the course of the tour.

I was shocked by the abject poverty of Soweto and the views of people like our tour guide. A few days later I was disappointed to hear Sean Fitzpatrick tell the New Zealand press how impressed he was with the changes in South Africa, regurgitating some of the statistics — like 'from 30 schools to 300 in Soweto' — we'd been told by our guide. In truth, the political situation wasn't much evolved at all and I think I would have said so if I'd been in Sean's shoes. (Little doubt there were political issues driving that message which we were not privy to.)

Everyone sort of fell into a particular role in the touring side, and right from the outset mine (along with a few others) was to cause a bit of shit and have a few laughs. A bit of humour was always welcome. One particular evening in Bloemfontein, I thought that the boys would appreciate it if I flogged the bus waiting for us outside training. I snuck out to the big car park, which was the size of four or five rugby fields. The bus driver had been silly enough to leave the keys in it (which reminded me of the uni campus), but he'd locked the door, so I crawled in through the side window. Our bus was the only bus in the car park, so I had plenty of dry, dirty ground to do a bit of paddock work in. When the boys came out, I was racing up and down, pulling the handbrake on, trying to get the 50-seater bus sideways — easier said than done.

Earle Kirton: He was good fun on tour. A delight. There was always fun around him. He lightened the load. Laurie could be quite dour, but we'd always get a laugh out of Ellis. It was bloody good, but I remember Sean Fitzpatrick taking me aside once and saying, 'Take that guy outside — if I see him jiggling and fidgeting once more while I'm trying to give a serious team talk, I'll yell at him'. That's just the way Lush is. He thinks he's expected to behave that way. He wasn't ill-disciplined, but he did his own thing, and was very shrewd and cunning about it.

Laurie Mains: Off the field he was always looking for the high jinks, but with his rugby he was very committed, very willing to play to a plan. He was always very responsible as a team member. In all the time I coached him, he never lacked discipline. He worked very, very hard as a rugby player. He was very fit. He never let me down. He was audacious at times, that might be the way I'd put it. He was even enigmatic in a way. He was capable of brilliant things when he had the chance.

South Africa was amazing in terms of the things we got to see. We went to diamond mines, gold mines, braais (barbecues) and big parties in the country. Everywhere we went we were treated to incredible hospitality and the locals bent over backwards to ensure we had the best time possible.

Our first game was against Natal in Durban. It was a big test and JK scored a beautiful try off a short pass from Frank Bunce. As one of the non-playing reserves I had to do a 'meet and greet' after the game, go around the braais in the car park (second only to Argentinean barbies), chatting to the rugby fans. It was beautiful weather and we enjoyed a few beers with the locals, until we heard a gunshot ring out in the car park. I found out later that a black man had pinched a chop off a barbecue and made a dash for freedom. The security guards, rather than just grabbing him and giving him a telling off, shot the poor guy in the back of the head, killing him. That really hammered home just how cheap life was there.

The test at Johannesburg's Ellis Park was cool — to sit in a crowd of over 70,000 people, watching the All Blacks beat the Springboks, was a real event.

We went to a safari park outside Johannesburg one afternoon, in a massive Iroquois chopper. It was a good 20-minute ride out there and the sliding doors of the chopper were open: one of the security guards had a hand gun and allowed a few pot-shots at the animals as we flew over the plains. It was a pretty loose sort of a scene, but fortunately we had shit-show of hitting anything from that far away.

We were convinced we would see the Big Five — buffalo, elephants, rhino, lions and leopards — and we jumped onto a jeep that had no sides, just a roll cage between us and the wild beasts for our safari (which was mildly disconcerting). As it happened, we saw bugger all, only a few animals from a long way off, and a couple of baboons hanging out of trees with their big pink arses, and a warthog or two.

Naturally, we started winding up the driver, calling the park a rock farm and demanding to see some lions. Little surprise that the black fella sitting on the front of the jeep drew the short straw and was sent off into the bushes to find some. There was no way you would have got me walking out into that hip-high grass, where the lions were very hard to spot, but this guy took off and started throwing stones into the bushes to scare the lions out into the open. The week before, the guide told us, a leopard had come down a tree and pinched one of the trackers and had a good munch. He survived, but only just. Before long some lions came ambling out and our tracker sprinted back to the jeep. We got our look at the lions, but we very easily could have been looking at something quite different.

On the way back we got out to look at the ostriches. Ostriches have long legs that bend backwards, and have been known to kill with a swift kick. The guide was busy telling us how dangerous they could be, when Loey snuck up on one and grabbed a big handful of its arse feathers. The thing let out this almighty 'Moo' and took off like a scalded cat at full speed, heading straight for me. 'Shit, that's the end of me,' I thought, as I took off.

I've never moved so fast. The bird was just a couple of steps behind me, so I went hard right in the hope that he couldn't turn corners. It worked, but the ostrich set its sights on Neil Gray, our manager, instead. Everyone was diving for cover and there, in the midst of it all, was Loey cracking up. He thought it was the funniest thing in the world. As far as Loey was concerned there had to be an element of danger for anything to be fun, and he happily provided all the danger, all of the time, on that tour.

All of the mid-weekers who weren't required for Saturday games — me, Eric Rush, Steve Bachop, Blair Larsen, Dallas Seymour, Mark Cooksley and a few others — took a night-time hunting trip to a game farm. When we got there we were told we were going to get to fire machine guns. We decided to have a few beers beforehand to calm the nerves, and as we were standing around, one of the guys, a big Boer who was taller than Mark Cooksley, proudly showed us how he could do a 'torpedo' with a can of beer. Of course, we had all seen and done torpedoes hundreds of times, but I told him I'd never seen one before. He was a bit of a show-off, going on about how quick he was at it, so I asked him if I could have a crack at one.

I sort of laboured my way through the setting-up process, asking him a couple of times how to do it, then whacked it in in about half the time he had. The Boer was horribly embarrassed and furious that his game had been ambushed by a pipsqueak, and challenged me to a competition. We had a dozen or so challenges and after every couple I excused myself for a toilet break, whipped behind a tree, and threw up so that I could be good for the next one. My opponent wasn't so smart and eventually keeled over and passed out. It was a real-life David-and-Goliath struggle. In the morning he was still lying prone by the bonfire.

After that the locals handed out the weapons and we set out for our shooting. It was like going off to war — there were machine guns, AK47s and hand grenades. Mark grabbed a machine gun, which had a range of three kilometres or something ridiculous, and pulled the trigger. The gun took off like a motor mower. Mark spun around with it and we all hit the deck and fortunately the guide managed to wrestle the gun off him before he shot everyone in the near vicinity.

You'd think that would be enough to put everyone off, but we all climbed on the back of a van and went out to shoot springbok. After such a rigorous start to the evening drinking with the big Boer, I was that pissed I couldn't hit anything and, to be fair, was in hugging and smiling mode — not ideal for killing (but from my hazy memory, the boys got a springbok and a warthog).

In Durban we had an afternoon off at a water park. Earle and Laurie decided to come along and have a bit of a crack — Laurie used to love getting into his Speedos, so he was very happy. We all jumped on rubber tubes and made a chain of about seven blokes, even though there were signs saying 'No Chaining'. Rushie was the first tyre and we really got moving on the way around the first corner. It was the same physics principle that applied on a rollercoaster: when the back catches up with the front it propels it down the slope and hard into the corner. Rushie was going so fast that when the second corner came along he was pushed off the slippery painted slide and onto the concrete path. He skinned his entire arse and back. It was one of the grizzliest skinnies I have ever seen (and only mildly funny because it was so horrible). Earle and Laurie hadn't seen what happened and Rushie knew he'd be in trouble for playing silly buggers, so he tried to hide his injuries. He had to go to the doctor and get made up with all sorts of dressings, and then play on a hard-as-rock ground a few days later covered in bandages.

Earle almost suffered the same fate, after asking me which was the slowest slide. Of course, I jerked him and sent him down the one that was almost vertical, a 200-metre drop.

I convinced him that because the water was coming down slowly, that was the beginners' one. Earle jumped in and gave himself a little push off, and being shaped like a bowling ball, took off down the slide. We started pissing ourselves as Earle disappeared over the precipice. A normal man got up to about 80 km/h on this particular slide, so Earle must have shot past doing the ton! When he knew he was in real trouble he turned back to look at me and started screeching, the profanities pouring from his mouth. We could hear the sound of his flesh burning on the way down, as he tried to stop himself with his arms.

Earle Kirton: He set me up. They all laughed and said it was easy. I got up there and it was like a luge. It was huge. 'Go with the flow, boy,' Marc was yelling. I tore all the skin off my knees, elbows and bum. It was terrible.

By the time he hit the water Earle had sucked in so much water he'd blown up to about twice his normal size. It was very visual and we were rolling around in absolute hysterics.

Earle Kirton: I was sore for days. Laurie thought it was bloody funny, but I told that little bugger Lush that he wouldn't play the next game.

Laurie Mains: I cracked up — I thought it was incredibly funny. I may have made a comment about being a bit more careful, but he wasn't punished.

I'll never forget him standing at the bottom of the slide shaking his fists at me. We found out later he'd put his back out. I was made a reserve for the next mid-week game, as punishment I think for having too much fun at a coach's expense, but it was well worth it. Even thinking about it now makes me laugh out loud.

Ric Salizzo: Marc was just so enthusiastic that occasionally he'd overstep the mark without realising.

There were several traditions at the end of every All Blacks tour then. One was that after the last game of the tour, once the players had changed into their Number Ones, everyone went around trying to rip each other's shirt pockets. And, as has been written about in other books, on the bus trip after that last game the new boys had to take on the back seat. I'm not sure why that happened, but there were some real big buggers at the back of the bus on that first tour — Mike Brewer, Loey, Fitzy, Zinny — so when the call went out to take them on it was a serious thing. We all put our mouth guards in and rushed down there. I locked in behind Jamie Joseph and Arran Pene; behind me was Stu Forster. It was a fairly aggressive scene.

My plan was to avoid Richard Loe: he was like a silver-backed gorilla and could have ripped my arm off with one hand if he wanted. He'd spent the first few weeks of the tour putting me in a headlock and ripping off the scab on my nose (which I'd got in a game in Australia) every time it started to heal. God bless him.

So I headed for Graham Purvis because Purvie was a friendly type of guy who was (hopefully) not going to hit as hard as some of the other guys down there. I chucked my head straight into his stomach and started trying to hook him from below. I was in an awkward position so he couldn't club me too hard, but when I heard 'Retreat', I stuck my head up and got a whack right on the nose. My leg was stuck under a seat so I had to yank it out to get free and took a good chunk out of it. The whole thing was over almost before it started, but there were bloody noses to be patched up and stitches to be sewn afterwards.

Loey and Jamie Joseph had a bit of a set-to in a bar that night. They'd been niggling at each other since the back-seat incident earlier in the day. Some of the rugby union officials were there and told Ric to break it up. Of course, he didn't — he would have been mad to get between those two — and somehow Loey fell and hit his head on a table and opened up a cut about 12 centimetres long. It was a beauty.

Loey was rushed off to the doctor's room, but Doc Mayhew, who was a hell of a good guy, was three sheets to the wind and couldn't be stirred. Being a rugged bugger and well anaesthetised Loey didn't worry too much about it and went off to bed. (Doc woke up in the morning and thought he'd been stabbed and robbed in the night because there was so much blood on him, the bed and carpet.)

The next morning we were all due on the bus at 9 a.m. for the drive to the airport. We were all on board at five to, but there was no Loey. Being late on the bus was a big no-no. You got fined, but not only that, if you did it too often you got it from the other boys and the management, and you could be dropped from the team. With the odd late night out celebrating, it was hard to get up on time sometimes, so you needed to rely on your roommate or find a friendly hotel concierge who would phone and wake you up.

Loey was an incredibly punctual guy, never late, so when it got to about five past we started to worry: he'd got a horrible whack on the head the night before — maybe he'd bled to death in the night.

Just as one of the boys was getting off the bus to check, out sauntered Loey. He was immaculate, beautifully turned out in his

Number Ones, his shoes polished, his tie straight. He looked perfect apart from a ragged lump of pillow foam perched on the top of his head. His head wound had bled in the night, sticking the pillow to it. He couldn't get himself unstuck, so he made do with cutting away as much of the pillow as he could and came out with a great big lump of foam attached to his head. Doc spent the next 45 minutes (much to our amusement) removing the foam from Loey's head and giving him about 30 stitches.

Our last night in South Africa we all sat around and had a few drinks and took turns making a team comment. Because we were the first official All Black team to tour South Africa for 16 years we had been considered a terrorism target and had a number of security guards who would sweep the bus for bombs and explosives every day and escort us everywhere we went. One security guard in particular, a red-headed chap called Kevin, I'll never forget. He was huge — we saw him lift a car that was blocking the bus by himself — and he loved to take the tops off his beer bottles with a cocked gun. He wasn't someone you wanted to mess with. When it was Kevin's turn that last night he said that he wished he had been able to shoot someone for us while we'd been on tour. In the politest possible way — you have to be careful when you're dealing with a half-shickered redhead toting a gun — we assured him that that wasn't necessary.

Later I had a drink with the black guys who had been our baggage handlers and assistants. That was one of the coolest moments for me. It was after the court session and there were only a few of us left in the room. The Otago boys and I played them one of my favourite songs, 'War' by Bob Marley. It's a song about freedom and the first line goes, 'Until the philosophy which holds one race superior and another inferior is finally and permanently discredited and abandoned everywhere is war'. We danced to it with these guys and shared a few beers. It was a very moving moment for me, to have a beer with these guys and see the glint they got in their eyes. It was something I'll never forget. I will get a chuckle if I go back on safari and see a black guy driving the jeep and a white fella sitting on the bonnet, chasing the odd lion out of the grass.

* * *

Nineteen ninety-three was, in terms of rugby, a great year for me. It started off with a trip to the Sevens in Palmerston North with the Otago team. A few of us, including Stu Forster, John Timu and me, were picked for the New Zealand Sevens side going to Hong Kong and we had a beaut time over there, playing footie and hooking up with the expat scene. A few varsity mates turned up to watch, as they always did, and still do, when the sevens are in town.

There were a few North Harbour guys in the team too and we all got on really well. Glen Osborne was good fun. He would flog absolutely everything out of the hotel room. Soaps, shampoos, cotton buds, sewing kits — you name it, it all went in his spare bag. Even the coffee sachets and the tea bags got pocketed. If he came to visit one of us, he'd fleece our rooms too. He'd leave and we'd realise we didn't have any toiletries left. I'm pretty sure he used to give it all to people at home as presents.

We were disappointed to lose against Samoa in the semi-final, but my overwhelming memory of that tournament is that I wished I was in the crowd enjoying a cold lager rather than running around the field. It was a unique party atmosphere.

JL and I worked well together during the 1993 NPC season and we flatted together too, in Castle Street. We had three seasons playing together as a centre/second-five combination for Otago and it was probably the best partnership I've had with anyone in any sport. By 1993 he was just starting to oust Arthur Stone from the second-five spot.

Every now and again Gordy would ask me who I would like to have at second-five that weekend, and I would always say JL. Then I'd have JL on; tell him that Gordy had asked, but that I'd had to say Arthur. I'd say, 'He's got just a bit more experience and I don't think it is going to do you any harm to spend some more time as his understudy'. He'd get so wound up, until Thursday, when he would be announced to play ahead of Arthur Stone.

The British and Irish Lions came to New Zealand that year and I didn't get picked for the All Blacks squad, but I did play in the Otago game against them. It was a fantastic game which we won — a huge result for us.

Towards the end of the NPC season, while we were in Hamilton, the All Blacks team for the tour to Britain was announced. John Timu and I made a pact that if we made the team we would shave our melons, and when we both got selected, Gordy set to with the clippers. The bowling ball suited JT, but I looked bloody awful and my mother was aghast.

Once again we had a good smattering of Otago boys in the All Blacks. Stu Forster joined us and Stephen Bachop took Grant Fox's place. Earle and Laurie thought that I might be able to make a go of first-five, the position I'd played as a schoolboy, and I was comfortable with that, so I was moved around.

Laurie Mains: In 1993 Marc did enough to convince me that he could be the test first-five. People like Gordy were prepared to give him enough rugby in that position, so he had enough under his belt by 1994.

Earle Kirton: Centre was too far out for him. He had short accelerated gas, not sustained gas. He and Jonah Lomu were by far the quickest players over a short distance, but as a centre he wasn't a great tackler, a hard enough tackler. He ran onto the ball and had great hands. I always felt he was a first-five. Laurie and I wanted him to go and play for King Country for a while as a first-five. He wouldn't go and he knew we were probably going to take him on tour anyway. He could have been a world-class first-five.

We went on tour to the United Kingdom, and in Britain we played a couple of early games, against England A at Gateshead and Scotland A in Glasgow. To play on grounds so steeped in tradition and so beautifully cared for lifted my game a wee bit, I think, and I went quite well. I was picked for the test against Scotland, which was a huge thrill.

Laurie Mains: He was very competitive, as was John Timu, and on the 1993 trip to the UK my fitness regime was that we worked hard during the week then rested before a game. Marc and JT were doing 100 sit-ups after practice. I spoke to them about that, told them not to do it. A few days later I saw them disappear around the back of the grandstand having their competition. I had to be careful about condoning his behaviour, but some things, like the sit-ups and that he was a fan of McDonald's, I let go.

In Edinburgh we stayed in a beautiful old place. While wandering around near Edinburgh Castle one day we came across a huge queue of people about a mile long. We asked someone what it was all about and discovered Muhammad Ali was inside doing a book signing. Ali was my absolute idol when I was young. My dad was a boxing referee in Wellington back in the early 70s and met Ali when he came to New Zealand. As a wee kid I sat in my parents' bed and watched Ali fight George Foreman on Mum and Dad's black-and-white TV. He remains in the top five people I'd most like to have been in the world (along with Tom Selleck, Frank Sinatra, Hugh Hefner and the Right Honourable Robert Nester Marley). I love boxing. It's like a game of chess: the art of self-defence is as important as hurting your opponent. It's a sport with no room for self-doubt and it's fascinating.

Ali was very cool in person, a huge man with huge charisma, even though he was showing symptoms of Parkinson's. He happily posed for a picture with me: he's holding his fist up and I'm wearing a daft grin.

The day before the Edinburgh test I was called to manager Neil Gray's room, along with the rest of the test team, and presented with my first test jersey. He handed me my shorts, my socks and my jersey, and I shook his hand. I took it all back to my room and put it on the chair by my bed, so when I woke up in the morning it was the first thing I saw. That was a cool feeling.

I was horribly nervous before the game. I was one of those guys who used to have to go to the toilet quite a lot before a game. I would literally walk out of the toilet, turn around and walk back in for another leak. Some guys would throw up; others would go right into themselves. It was just part of the nerves, the process. In my experience, when I'm nervous, I perform well. I'm in the right zone and focused.

Before the game we went out for a look around Murrayfield. It was enormous. I knew I had some friends in the crowd, three of my great mates from Wellington. It was Jeff Wilson's and Stu Forster's first tests too, so the three of us debuted together. Stu had a boomer of a game. I managed to get the first try of the game, so that broke the ice a bit, and another in the second half. Goldie got three superb tries and we finished up with a record win against Scotland.

When we returned to England I met another superstar, Lady Diana, Princess of Wales. The All Blacks and the English team had been invited to go and meet the Queen and Princess Anne. Naturally, we were all quite honoured and excited about it, and we headed off to Buckingham Palace, done up in our Number Ones, where we were met by an official royal chaperone. He was dressed to the nines — white gloves and the whole bit — and as he walked us into the hall he explained in a very plummy posh voice all the protocols that we were to follow in the presence of the Queen.

It wasn't the first time I'd met the Queen. HRH had come to Wellington when I was a schoolboy and all the boys from Wellington College went along to see her open the Mary Potter Hospice. We lined the driveway as she walked down smiling and waving and for some unknown reason she stopped at me and picked me out of the crowd to have a natter with.

'Tell me, young man', she said, 'what fundraising have you been doing for the Hospice?' I thought, 'Oh shit, I haven't done any fundraising'. So I lied. I told her I'd done bike-a-thons and cake-making-a-thons and every other bloody a-thons I could think of. She said, 'Oh, well done young man' and went on her way. I felt a bit bad about that, and it was a hard ask looking at the Queen's mug on the dollar note afterwards, knowing I'd given her the jimmy.

The chaperone showed us the door the Queen would come through, how to greet her, etc., and we were told to get into groups of five or so, so she could make her way around us chatting. We were allowed canapés, but no booze (very wise), and under no circumstances, the chaperone explained, was there to be any yahooing or loud noise at all. Then he said, 'And by the way, Diana, Princess of Wales will join the Queen', and the whole place just erupted with cheers.

Eventually the Queen and Princess Di arrived. The Queen came around to our group saying, 'Hello, thank you so much, blah, blah,

blah', and all I could think was, 'Please push off so we can talk to Princess Di'.

Finally, the Princess came over. To say she was the most beautiful person I'd ever seen in my life is a bit of an understatement. She was stunning, more beautiful than Elle Macpherson, and she had such a presence, a way of carrying herself, and an aura that was quite astounding and hard to explain really.

We were all trying to keep cool, but some did a better job than others. Liam Barry, who was actually quite an articulate chap, became completely tongue-tied and acted like a fool. I did my best and broke the ice with, 'You're quite tall. You must be about five foot 10 inches.'

'Actually, I am five foot 11 inches,' she said.

'Ah, only an inch shorter than me,' I said, which was quite obviously an exaggeration and gave her a laugh.

I then asked where Di might suggest I go skiing after the tour, as I had seen shots of her on the slopes in magazines. I conceded that I did not have her financial means and her recommendation (which I later took) was northern Italy, which she assured me was much cheaper than France.

We got on to the subject of the paparazzi and I took it upon myself to apologise for the photos a Kiwi gym owner had taken of her working out, and sold to newspapers right around the world. I followed up by asking if the paparazzi followed her everywhere, even out to dinner.

'Why?' she asked. 'Are you asking me out on a date?'

I had two options: to clam up like Liam Barry; or to act like any red-blooded Kiwi male should and say, as I did, 'As a matter of fact, that I am Princess'.

Back on the bus everyone gave me all sorts of shit. Liam Barry admitted that after my comments he'd apologised to Di for my forwardness and apparently she said, 'I would have gone, but it could only have been for a quick sandwich!'.

If only I'd known. (She was still married to old Chuck at that stage, but like most guys, I thought I could back myself in a competition with Big Ears.) I could have gone out with a princess. It could have been the beginning of something beautiful!

Flying Fijians and Poisoned Fruit

Three days after the visit to Buckingham Palace the All Blacks faced England at Twickenham. England played well. They dominated our forwards and put us under a huge amount of pressure. Matt Cooper had been injured in the test against Scotland and Eroni Clarke replaced him. Coops had been a good field-kicking option to back me up, but Eroni was more of a confrontational player. Against England we required a very accurate kicking game. Unfortunately, I came unstuck. I wasn't as accurate as Grant Fox and I kicked a few that went astray. We lost the game.

It was a real disappointment to have come all that way only to lose to England by so little. If there's one team the All Blacks hate to lose to — even more than Australia — it's England, and that's because they tend to be bloody arrogant winners. The New Zealand public found it hard to accept. Goldie blamed himself because he'd missed a few kicks, but it wasn't his fault. England just played bloody well and that was the way it went on the day. If we'd played them again the next week we likely would have beaten them. I copped a lot of the blame for having a fairly inaccurate day with the boot and that was a prick of a feeling.

Ric Salizzo: He was always seen as a really precocious talent. He had a fantastic sidestep. He had a huge range of skills. He had a blinder of a first game against Scotland in 1993. Then they lost against England and he got slammed.

In the changing rooms at Twickenham there are great big communal baths, beautiful hot baths you can have a soak in after a game, but on that afternoon we just couldn't enjoy it. Everyone was down; some of the guys even had a tear or two in their eyes. Neil Finn (who was at the game) joined us in the changing room with his guitar and played a few songs. The musically gifted Polynesian boys joined in.

At the official dinner that night the Poms gloated. It was a difficult evening, and the next day Will Carling was in all the papers saying it was England's 'greatest win'. We had to pick ourselves up, 'dump it and move on', in time for the Barbarians game at Cardiff the following week. It was an important game for us and we managed to come through with a good win there.

In those days no one played rugby for the money. We got a per diem of £22, which wasn't a fortune, but felt like it when it was handed out in one lump sum at the beginning of the trip and it was all the spending money I needed. We got to stay in nice hotels and all our meals were taken care of.

At the end of that particular tour we got a huge cash bonus for an exhibition game in Italy. We flew into Rome and travelled on to Venice, where the game was played. I think we were paid about $7000 for just one game. It was my first taste of professionalism and I thought it was brilliant. I used the money to go off travelling around Europe with Mandy.

After the game we went out for a big team dinner. Mandy was with me and after plenty of red wine over dinner, she started to feel a bit ill. I took her outside for a walk in the fresh air, but by the time we were ready to rejoin the others, we were lost. I knew the banquet hall was down an alleyway, but all the doors looked exactly the same and we couldn't find the right one back into the banquet hall. Eventually, we gave up. I had no idea how to find the hotel the team was staying in, so we checked into a nearby hotel.

The next morning we were feeling slightly the worse for wear and no clearer on how we were going to find the others. All I knew was that we had to take a boat, a train and a bus to get to our hotel. And we had about three hours to get back there before we were due to fly out.

After much more aimless wandering we found the alleyway we had come from the night before and after knocking on every door, found the banquet hall. I can't speak Italian, so I tried to explain as best I could that we'd been there the night before and lost the team. After much to-ing and fro-ing, the people there drew us a makeshift map and we managed to get home just in time.

* * *

I was just starting to feel comfortable at first-five in 1994 when I got injured in Palmerston North playing against Fiji for the New Zealand Universities team. It was always a hell of a good time, being away with the Universities side, because we were all young guys who liked to have a laugh, and we had Jock Hobbs (who liked to have fun as much as the rest of us) in charge.

The game was going pretty well, until I was head-butted by a flying Fijian in a late tackle. The guy's head went straight into my thigh and it bloody hurt. I knew straight away it wasn't good and within five minutes of being carried off the field my leg was so swollen I couldn't bend it much past five degrees.

The doctors had a look at it, told me to put a bit of ice on it, keep it elevated, and get an early night. When I woke up the next morning, I couldn't move at all. My thigh was as tight as a hot sausage: if I'd stuck a fork in it, it probably would have popped.

I was in real agony, so much so that I thought my leg might be broken, but I had to get back to Dunedin, so the Otago contingent got on one of those pencil-case planes headed for Christchurch. As the plane rose and the altitude got higher, the pain deep in the muscle got worse. It was unbearable. I lay down on the floor of the plane and watched the second hand on my watch go round, second by second, for an hour and a half, until we landed in Christchurch, where an ambulance met me. To this day it's the most pain I have ever been in.

After various tests and X-rays I was diagnosed with a very serious haematoma. My leg was absolutely poked for about two months. I spent weeks in rehab, trying to get the thing better, and I missed my opportunity to string a couple of seasons together playing first-five.

While I was waiting for my leg to heal I got a call from a Maori fella who said he had a cure, a way to draw out the haematoma. I was to go and peel some bark off a kowhai tree, put the bark in a very hot bath and then soak in it. My flatmates thought I had lost the plot when they came home to find me soaking in brown water. The trick didn't work and I was stained brown from chest to toe for about two weeks.

Ric Salizzo: When Earle Kirton suggested he go to first-five everyone thought he was mad. At the beginning of the next season, when Marc needed to carry on his growth, he got injured, and he didn't have that opportunity to prove everyone wrong. It would have been really interesting to see how he developed as a first-five.

I wasn't able to play for the All Blacks when the Springboks toured New Zealand in 1994 and that was probably my chance to have a crack at making the first-five test position my own. In my absence they tried several players: Stephen Bachop, Simon Mannix and Jon Preston.

Laurie Mains: I would dispute that other players were better at first-five. In 1994 we struggled in that position and that's why we brought in Andrew Mehrtens. My own view is that Marc had all the abilities of Andrew Mehrtens. He was every bit as talented a player.

I did come right though, in time to play for Otago against the Boks. It was a dreadful day, pouring with rain, but there was a massive Carisbrook crowd. The Springboks had played Auckland and Waikato, but no one had managed to knock them over. We were the ninth provincial side to play them and we were keen to get the mounted springbok head that the Boks bring with them. The head is awarded to the first provincial team to beat the touring Springbok team and there is only one per tour, so they are highly valued.

The Springboks fielded a full-strength side and, despite being a converted try down in the first few minutes, we managed to beat them. We were rapt when we won — to do that the year after beating the Lions was pretty bloody cool — and it was a thrill to be back on the field after so long. The Springbok head now hangs at Carisbrook, although it has been stolen on one or two occasions for a series of very odd photos.

* * *

Before the All Blacks trials in 1995 I started to think about selection for the World Cup. Jonah Lomu had hit the scene and commandeered one wing position, while Goldie had made the other his own. Glen Osborne was doing well at fullback. Andrew Mehrtens had outstanding skills. I needed to be in top form.

Around that time I was approached by Ian Robson about playing for the Warriors. I thought about it, but I wanted to play in the World Cup first, and make a decision thereafter. It was not the first league offer I'd had. In 1992, Graham Lowe had asked if I'd consider playing for Manly, but that was out of the question at that time.

Ric Salizzo: I was a big believer in how good Macca was. Before the World Cup in 1995, there were whispers that he was going to go to league. I rang him up and asked him what was going on. He explained he had to look at offers because he didn't know if he was going to make the All Blacks again. After his injury he probably thought, 'I can't rely on rugby for my future'. I called Laurie up and told him Macca could be another Campese. Then I called Marc back and told him he was very much in the picture.

At the All Blacks trial I was put in the Possibles team and I marked Jonah. I knew I had to get up on Jonah as quickly as possible: I couldn't leave any room for him to get the ball, but the moment he did I had to tackle him and cling to his ankles for dear life. Jonah is enormous — tackling him was akin to a 14-year-old tackling a grown man — so I had to hit him perfectly, bang on, otherwise he would go over me and it would really, really hurt.

As it happened, the ball didn't really roll our way that day and Jonah managed to get a couple of tries. I got picked for the All Blacks in that old utility position again. It was a bit of a frustration, but it did mean that I was one of the first picked for the World Cup touring team because I could cover a few positions.

Jock Hobbs: His versatility was his strength, but it counted against him too. He got a reputation for that versatility and it became a limitation. If others had allowed him to gain momentum in the role of first-five, he could have done very well.

We were all pretty focused on winning by the time we left for South Africa. We were super fit (I don't think I have ever been as fit as I was then), so finely tuned that we knew no other team would be as fit as us, and we left New Zealand in a really positive frame of mind.

It's a massive trip to South Africa, but we got off the plane in Johannesburg, got to our hotel and got our training gear on. The medical advice was that we needed to have at least 48 hours acclimatising to the high altitude and getting over the travel before we trained, but Laurie made us train straight away. That was horrendous. He slogged us for an hour and a half doing 'down and ups', saying, 'Switch on boys, this is not a bloody holiday, we're here to do the business'.

By the end of it our lungs were burning, some of the guys even vomited blood, but we knew exactly how mentally tough Laurie wanted us.

During the first game, against Ireland, Goldie got injured and I went on (Goldie's my mate, but I was pretty pleased about that). The hard South African grounds always suited my style of play, free-running, open rugby. I thought that I might be able to get a few games if I played well.

We moved through our first two pool games relatively comfortably and met Japan in Bloemfontein. Laurie put me at centre, so I got my first and only test in the number 13 jersey, my favourite position. Coincidentally, before the game I'd read the programme and seen that the World Cup record for tries by an individual was four. That stuck in my head.

We were off to a good start even before the game began — when we did the haka the Japanese looked terrified, some of them even started crying. And we gave them a thumping. The forwards played really well and Simon Culhane had a magnificent kicking game. The ball came my way and I got three tries in the first half.

John Leslie: He rang me from South Africa the day of the World Cup game against Japan. I said, 'Give me the Bob Marley salute if you score. You can see in the television footage of that game he does it — his hand's in a fist up by his head when he gets up after a try.'

I knew I had a sniff at the World Cup record and after halftime I got another try, and knew my name was going into the record books. Then I went on to get two more tries before fulltime. I was pretty happy with myself, but as soon as I got into the changing rooms, I got an absolute bagging from Laurie. He thought there were a couple of occasions when I could have passed the ball to someone else.

Laurie Mains: There were a couple of times when he could have passed the ball, given someone else an easy run over the line. His play worked against Japan, but it wouldn't have worked against better sides. Having said that, we were very proud that Marc had broken the record. He did display some brilliance on that day, as he was prone to do.

Laurie was right, I probably should have passed the ball, but Goldie got three tries that day, and others got the odd ones too, and on those occasions I could have passed I scored the tries. I was 23 and in the best form of my life, and I was probably a bit selfish. Laurie tore strips off me for it, but that's OK, he loved getting stuck into people every now and then.

Earle Kirton: He annoyed me then too. He got caught short of the line once. He'd scored a lot of tries and he should have off-loaded. There were a lot of pursed lips after that.

John Leslie: I wasn't surprised he got into trouble for not passing — that comes with going for world records.

The World Cup is an intense environment to be a part of, and I grabbed any chance to relieve the tension. Our security guards were a good bunch of blokes, and they'd given a few of us their police badges to carry around. I kept one inside my wallet and used to flash it around when we were out for the night. It was very handy for queue-jumping at nightclubs and getting free beer. I made the mistake of asking one girl for her ID so I could get her name for one of the single fellas. Her boyfriend one-upped me by peeling back his jacket to reveal a gun and I had to make a hasty retreat.

The guards also ordered us commando outfits, which arrived the day we were to play Scotland in the quarter-final. Andrew Mehrtens and I were so excited, we had everything from a green beret to the army boots. We chucked all the kit on and tore up and down the corridor doing forward rolls and bursting into other guys' rooms. I burst into the physio room and cocked my pretend finger-gun, ready to drill a round into somebody, and ran straight into Laurie. An hour before we were due to get on the bus to play the semi-final of the World Cup and Mehrts and I were running around playing war games — even though he had a good sense of humour, that went down like a cup of cold sick with 'Lozza'.

Goldie was still crook when we played Scotland, so I started that game. The Scots were quite hard on defence and really gave it their all, but they were outclassed and we won comfortably. Then we came up against England, the bastards who had beaten us in 1993, in the semi-final. That was one the All Blacks really wanted to win. I was a reserve that day and it was a pleasure to watch the Poms get beaten. Jonah had an unbelievable game and the whole team played extremely well and we went into the final of the World Cup well and truly the favourites to win.

About 72 hours out from the final I started to feel really crook. I was lethargic, nauseous, and before long I started to vomit. Soon, I was going at both ends. When a couple of the other boys fell ill as well, Laurie quarantined us at the far end of the hotel so we wouldn't pass on whatever we had to the rest of the team. The team doctor also kept an eye on us.

By the next day, Friday, 22 of the boys were sick with food poisoning. I had started to feel ever so slightly better (probably because I'd been one of the first to go down) and those of us who could went for a light run, but I almost fainted when I tried a 100-metre sprint. A team meeting was called to discuss our options. Should we announce we were sick and say we wouldn't play the final? Should the game be postponed? Should the team be tested to see what had made us all ill? Eventually, it was decided that we would play South Africa the following day. Nothing would be said about the food poisoning, we'd be stoic about it. Postponing the game, Laurie said, would be seen as defeatist.

On the way to the game the bus stopped by a group of South African supporters. They were going berserk. 'We're going to kill you, you black bastard,' they yelled at Jonah. It was disconcerting to say the least. At the stadium there were 90,000 people waiting for us in the stands. When Nelson Mandela led the South African anthem, it was quite overwhelming.

Goldie came off with about 25 minutes left in the game and I was sent on. Even though a lot of the guys were still really crook, at fulltime we were level with South Africa. We played another 10 minutes each way, which was torture thanks to the state we were in. How the guys who fell ill 18 hours after me played 100 minutes of rugby I don't know; it must have been sheer bloody-mindedness. I dropped a couple of passes in that game. My hands were something I'd never had to worry about — they were the easiest part of the game for me — but on that day I missed two balls in succession. It wasn't the pressure; I guess I just wasn't at my best.

In extra time a dropped-goal attempt by Mehrts narrowly missed. Then the South African flyhalf kicked a droppie that went over, and our fate was sealed. We had played our hearts out, but it hadn't been enough. We got pipped at the post by an inferior side.

Everyone was devastated. Not only because we'd lost, but because of how we'd lost. We'd been expected to win, and hadn't, and now we couldn't say why. If we put our hands up and said, 'We were poisoned', we'd look like poor sports. So we had to come back to New Zealand and take the criticism on the chin.

Later it came out that we thought we'd been poisoned intentionally. In the whole six-week tour only five people fell ill, until 48 hours before the World Cup final, when 22 went down. I think someone probably injected the fruit in our team room. The All Blacks management were fastidious about what we ate — we weren't allowed to eat outside our hotel — but we used to have fruit bowls in our team room and after training everyone would go and grab a piece of fruit. Or it could have been the coffee and tea. The South Africans mocked us when that theory came out, but I think that's what happened. It certainly wasn't a coincidence that we all got sick just before the game, and I have no doubt that if we had been 100 per cent fit we would have come home with the World Cup in 1995.

Afterwards the team went to Australia for the Bledisloe Cup and that's where the meetings with the World Rugby Corporation took place. The WRC was Kerry Packer's idea, a kind of rebel rugby union. They were talking about paying $500,000 per player, so the boys all looked very seriously at going with them.

Ric Salizzo: It was a really funny time. The WRC people were going to offer him a really huge contract. He was one of a handful of guys in the top tier as far as they were concerned. They saw a big life for him off the field as well as on. At the time I couldn't see it.

Joining the WRC would have meant no All Blacks jersey, no national or regional pride. In a way it meant selling out the All Blacks jersey and all that it stood for. It was something that I was happy not to be a part of really: I'd already decided to sign up with the Warriors.

Jock Hobbs: I was in negotiations with the players on behalf of the Rugby Union. Marc kept to himself and was quite quiet, because he had other options — league being one of them. I met with him and his father and said that Marc was valued and wanted by the New Zealand Rugby Union but, unfortunately, from a New Zealand Rugby Union perspective, he decided to go to league. It was disappointing, but I respected that that was what Marc wanted to do.

Chris Ellis: After he finished his university studies in 1995 I rang him up and I said, 'I've got a job for you, the money's pretty good, but you'll have to give up being an

All Black'. Of course it was the Warriors offer, but I didn't tell him that at that stage. He said, 'No problem'. The ease with which he surrendered his All Black jersey surprised me, but he is of a different generation. In my generation, if you were an All Black, you were one for life.

Ric Salizzo: To really be the best in the world you have to want it more than anyone else. Maybe in the end he didn't want that; maybe there were other things he wanted. There were more things going on in his brain. Obviously, that shaped his future and influenced his decision to go to rugby league.

It was incredible to watch the negotiations and witness some of the 'logic' that was coming out of Sydney. Guys were being blinded by the dollars. I learnt a couple of valuable business lessons there: it's amazing what money will make a man do; and, you can seldom trust people when there's money involved.

That the deal fell through is to the credit of Jock Hobbs, Josh Kronfeld and Jeff Wilson. Jock Hobbs managed to get Goldie and Josh to commit to the All Blacks. They were two big parts of the All Blacks equation, and the first to stick with the NZRU.

In hindsight I think the WRC threat was a good thing for New Zealand rugby. The rugby union was fairly draconian in terms of its approach to the players in those days, perhaps because it knew the players didn't have other options, or maybe because there was a lack of commercial nous. The Rugby Union had to act quickly to mend that once the WRC came along.

Funnily enough, the logic behind joining the Warriors was primarily a loyalty thing for me. Moving to league gave me the chance to make a clean break from playing rugby in New Zealand, and playing against my mates in Otago. I'd had five years in Dunedin and finally finished my degree, so if I wanted to start my career, I had to leave. I still had a few years of playing footie left, but a start in the business world meant a move to Auckland and potentially playing rugby for Auckland. I didn't want to do that — play against Otago in an Auckland team. Otago was the only rugby team that I ever really cared about, and I didn't want to jump the fence.

There was a Speight's Southern Man song that Peter Kean, our Lion Breweries liaison man, used to sing in the Otago court sessions. It goes: 'Some of the boys got it into their head about moving up north, follow the bread. But that ain't for me, that kind of thing just don't rate. This is one Southern Boy who's not crossing the Strait.' I was about to do just that.

The other incentive to go to league was financial. The Super League had just come in and the Australian Rugby League was vying for players. It was offering massive cash incentives and one-off tax-free payments to tempt rugby players to come across to league.

Earle Kirton: It was a commercial decision. We lost the talent of the bugger and he hadn't reached his potential — I thought as he got older he would have got better and better. I didn't think he was ever going to make a success of league with all the tackles involved. I didn't know how he would cope with that. But it set him up. He used his brains and it led to a more than adequate income.

My last game for Otago was the NPC final against Auckland. It was really hard for me to play that last game and not tell anyone it was my last. It went against the whole team ethos of trust and loyalty, but I wasn't allowed to go public about joining the Warriors yet. Sitting in the changing room for the last time, knowing that I wouldn't be coming back and not being able to share that with the guys — that was difficult. It would have been so nice to be able to say, 'Hey, this is my last game — thanks for everything', but I had to play along with the politics. When, not long after, it came out that I was going to the Warriors, I felt like I had betrayed the team a wee bit.

Ric Salizzo: I was sad he left rugby when he did. He could have gone on to do all sorts of wonderful things. But he got to be an All Black and then saw all the windows that were open to him.

At the end of 1995 there was an All Blacks tour to Italy, but I couldn't go because I hadn't signed with the Rugby Union. I was really, really keen to go — I would have loved to have had another couple of tests for the All Blacks, but it wasn't to be and I was left biding my time until I started with the Warriors in 1996.

In all the All Blacks tours I went on, there was never any player who was a dickhead. They were all good guys in their own way. Some of them I was tighter with than others, but all of them were good guys, guys you'd like to have a beer with.

Laurie Mains: The players with high spirits, that's part of their personality and a part of why they're a great rugby player. To get the best out of those sorts of players isn't always easy but Marc played to the best of his abilities. I did love his spirit and cheekiness. And he wasn't just an All Black, but also a very good test player. He never reached the heights in rugby. If he'd stayed in rugby he would have continued to have a very strong career. While he was a successful league player, it wasn't a game that gave him the opportunities rugby gave him. League is a less intricate game and that's another reason it didn't suit him.

Ric Salizzo: I think he worked harder at being a rugby player than he admits sometimes. He's always had a great work ethic with his football. He was a very good rugby player and he got a lot of enjoyment out of it. He worked really, really hard to get to the top, because you have to.

I'm not sure that I could ever class myself as a good All Black, of achieving the goal I set myself in 1992 when I first became an All Black. A good All Black is somebody who has played heaps of tests and done everything right. I had only a handful of tests. For the time I was there, I was alright, but it certainly wasn't the lengthiest or most exemplary of All Black careers. The decision to go to league, just as rugby was turning professional, was definitely the right one, but I often wondered how many All Black tests I could have got to if I had hung around.

Switching Codes

Iwas happy to move to Auckland in 1996. The further south you go the more disdain people have for Auckland. In Otago it was the done thing to bad-mouth Auckland — even the Aucklanders started disliking Auckland when they moved down there — but Auckland's a fantastic place. There's a bit of bravado and a bit of brashness and there's some showiness, but I think there is in any big city. I like that I can go surfing, diving, boating or mountain biking much of the year and, most importantly, I have plenty of mates from school and varsity in Auckland. That makes any city great.

My challenge was moving from amateur sportsman to professional. The Warriors had signed some big names, including John Kirwan, and it was an exciting new time for league. I was really impressed with the way Ian Robson ran the Warriors as a business. He's a shrewd guy and in those early days he was certainly able to drum up some huge support in terms of crowd numbers.

I'd made a clean break with rugby and I was looking forward to ripping into league and giving it a crack. The Warriors were really supportive in terms of my desire to begin a business career and organised a job for me at KPMG as a marketing assistant, so I could get some work experience.

I was a bit nervous about how rugby league was going to be in terms of the physical aspect of it and whether or not the culture would be similar to rugby union. Physically, I had to combine both strength and fitness and for the first time I really started doing weights. Weights were not a part of the All Blacks equation in the amateur days. You were told to get in shape and that meant keeping fit, and training was important, but most of the size and strength the players had back then was natural. Now rugby players spend as much time as the league guys, if not more, in the gym.

At our first weights trial we had to bench press as much as we could for one press. Guys like Gene Ngamu and Matthew Ridge were doing up to 120–130 kilograms. The best I could get out was 95 kilograms. I was so hellishly embarrassed by that. I thought I was fit coming out of the World Cup.

Edgar, our trainer, was an ex-gridiron weights coach, and used to train the buggery out of us. Every day was the same: get up, have breakfast, go to the gym and do weights, come home sore as anything to have lunch and a quick sleep, get back up for afternoon training (and train into the ground), have dinner, then back to sleep. My cousins, who I stayed with before I went flatting, couldn't believe how anti-social I was — any time off was spent in bed! I've never been so sore, but after a month or so I'd broken through the pain barrier.

There were a couple of drugs being bandied around in the Warriors in those days to help us with our strength. There was creatine monohydrate, a supplement which increased your muscle mass and helped you retain water. Theoretically, if you got hit, creatine monohydrate made it easier to recover from the impact. Some of the guys started creatine-loading in pre-season and they would literally start growing in front of our eyes. The challenge for those big fellas was to get the balance between taking the hits and being fit enough to last 80 minutes. I was one of those guys who always wanted to put on weight and never could (even now I'm the same weight I was when I was playing professionally). I tried creatine every now and then, but I always stayed exactly the same weight.

The next big thing was a Bulgarian drug called Trebistan, which increased testosterone levels by some astronomical amount. Bobby Lanigan, who was a good bugger and our fitness trainer, would say, 'Right-oh boys, into the Trebistan,' and he'd hand out trays of the stuff. Guys would start loading it two days out from a game, and it made them much more aggressive (and incredibly amorous too). Some of them used to get quite fired up on the stuff. It didn't make any sense to me. The drug came from the Eastern Bloc and it was something that the weightlifters over there used, but I told Bobby I'd take it only if he could show me the research that proved it did no harm. He never did, so I never took it.

I was on the wing in my first game for the Warriors. Illawarra put the ball wide when they were on attack and the ball bobbled off somebody's shoulders and popped straight into my hands, and so with my first touch of the ball I got a 90-metre runaway and scored under the posts. 'This league's looking like a bit of me,' I thought.

Earle Kirton: When he went to league I ran into John Monie at a cocktail party. He asked me, 'What's the story with Marc Ellis?'. I said to him, 'You have to look after him a bit — he's not as rough and tough as Matthew Ridge. He's a more subtle guy.' He said, 'He's one of the best ball players I've ever seen'. I agreed. He had great hands.

Matthew Ridge, ex-All Black, ex-Kiwi, television presenter: He was very quick and instinctive and if he got some space he could outpace anyone. He could get knocked around a bit. I think the ferocity of league surprised him. That took a bit of getting used to, as it did for me.

League is a great game to watch. It's 80 minutes and it's non-stop. The biggest challenge for me was all the different angles you have to run. You learn from the age of five in a game of rugby where you're meant to be if you want to score a try, but in league you have to be in different places and you have to understand three or four phases ahead of time where the play is going to be made. There were all these calls, and they'd be called three in advance. I'd find that I was sprinting around in the background trying desperately to link up with the ball and failing miserably nine times out of 10. That was something I struggled with.

I didn't get much guidance either, in terms of anyone telling me where exactly to position myself to get on the end of some of those phase plays. It's something that comes naturally if you've played league your whole life, in the same way that it comes naturally in rugby union, but I found it pretty trying. The only bit of advice John Monie gave me in my first year was about three games before the end of the season. 'Am I doing anything right or wrong?' I asked him. 'You're going all right, just don't go over the bloody sideline,' was his reply. (To be honest, I had flirted with the chalk a little too much. In rugby the sideline's your friend — in league it's your enemy.) That was it. I didn't get coached any more than that.

Matthew Ridge: I don't think Marc got the coaching he needed, the help. He was left to his own devices. I think he found that quite hard. I don't think we saw the best of Marc as a league player, that's for sure. That had to do with him being thrown in the deep end a bit. Consequently, his enjoyment factor wasn't there.

I was a bit disappointed in that and I think if John had spent a bit more time communicating with me I might have been a bit more effective in those first couple of years. With the benefit of hindsight I should have asked more questions, rather than going with the flow.

John used to like to single out players and criticise them. One day he came into the changing room and called Phil Blake a coward for shying away from a tackle. Blake had played for years at the top, had been one of the greatest players in league in his heyday, and he was being bagged by the coach in front of all the other players. I thought that was a very negative way to deal with the players, quite different from my experience in rugby, and I don't think it got the best out of people. Our ability to play at form was hamstrung by a coach who used to take shots at guys in public.

When we played the big teams, like the Brisbane Broncos, we went all right, because there was no pressure on us. We were expected to lose, so we were free to throw everything at it and make the odd mistake through trying hard. We didn't worry too much about it. When we played the teams that were inferior, players clammed up because the

Coldstarts — where you invited someone you had never met along to a flat dinner — were a licence for depravity. This shot must have been taken very early on . . .

Enjoying a beer and a game of pool with some West Coasters.

In the 'tent village' after an All Blacks test at Carisbrook.

Horse riding with Mandy somewhere in Fiji.

Black Flag won't kill these ones . . .

Enjoying a quiet one with good mates Andrew, Dave, Rich and Lindon.

Waffle and I enjoying a 'Stefan's Orange Juice' after another night under the stars.

Flatmates Waffle and Billy pose proudly just after we'd signed the lease on 663 Castle Street.

Not quite sure what should be written here . . .

The Otago team of the early '90s included the best bunch of guys I ever played with.

Me, Paul Cooke, Steve Bachop, Stu Forster and John Leslie.

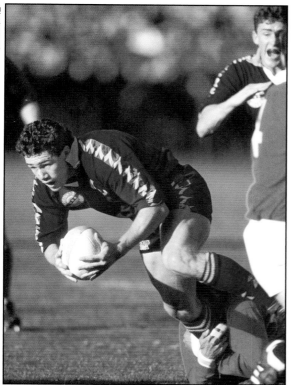

In action for Otago against the British and Irish Lions in 1993. We won the match 37–24.

The things you do when you're drunk . . .

We've just beaten what was effectively the 1994 Springboks' test line-up — it was probably my greatest result in an Otago jersey.

Giving ref Colin Hawke an earful after he'd awarded Auckland a dubious penalty try in the NPC first division final of 1995. The try effectively handed Auckland the title. This was my last game for Otago.

Me and Arran Pene.

My university mates supporting their beloved Hawke's Bay. We thumped them, from memory.

My mate Sam Williams.

Looking to offload to John Timu in my first test, against Scotland at Murrayfield in 1993.

Peter Bush

Everything went right against Japan at the 1995 World Cup. Well, that's everything until I got off the field and copped a serve from Laurie Mains.

Ellis Collection

Goldie and me freshening up for the night ahead after a World Cup match in '95.

Ellis Collection

The evening of the 'Torpedo Incident'. My opponent was the size of All Black Mark Cooksley (foreground).

Lining up in my first game for the Warriors in 1996.

pressure was on, we weren't confident and we weren't mentally in the right space. As it turned out we had a pretty average season in 1996, with 10 wins and 11 losses.

Off the field there were plenty of high jinks, of course. That January, while we were still in pre-season training, I went down to the Wellington Cup to catch up with a few Wellington mates. The Wellington Cup is always a great day — we'd get dressed up and go for a bit of gambling.

Things were going beautifully: it was a warm day and we were enjoying a few quiets. Then a guy came over, an official, and asked if I'd ride the Clerk of the Course's horse out before the next race. I told him I'd love to and that I'd had plenty of horse-riding experience — high-country mustering etc. — which couldn't be further from the truth. I don't know what I was thinking. Horses scare the hell out of me.

Sure enough he brought it along and I got stuffed into a jockey's outfit and put on the horse, a big grey thing with a pot-belly that certainly didn't look as if it was made for speed. I was supposed to walk along slowly, leading out the horses to be warmed up for the next race, then break left and walk my horse back in. As I came ambling out I got a rather tepid response from the crowd. That soon changed.

Once the racehorses started to warm up on the track my horse got very excited. I didn't know how to control it and pandemonium broke loose. It took off down the straight. I yanked the reins, yelling, 'Stop, stop'. The horse kept bolting. By the time we reached the end of the straight my nag had passed all bar one of the racehorses, and I was holding onto the saddle for dear life.

I was headed right for the last horse and jockey and I had no idea how to turn the horse, so I screamed at the jockey to get out of the way. The jockey looked up just as I abandoned ship and jumped off my horse. I fell in a heap on the ground as my horse collided with the other horse, knocking the jockey off his mount. Everyone in the stands started cheering and screaming and yelling.

I knew I had really cocked up: I'd got a standing ovation from the crowd, but I'd delayed TV coverage of the race and injured the favoured horse for the next race. And, John Monie was a mad-keen gambler and he loved the Wellington Cup, so I was in no doubt that he would have been watching (when I got back to training John had a laugh about it, luckily). I'm sure Wellington racing officials never asked anyone to do that again.

When the 1996 league season finished I went to Thailand with a few mates on holiday. One night I got a call in the hotel room from Frank Endacott, who asked me to come back and play for the Kiwis. I had asked Frank prior to going to Thailand whether there was a chance I would be required. He said it was unlikely, so I ripped into a very social holiday indeed. When I got his call I was rapt and came straight back, but I was a little worried about how my fitness had suffered from two weeks in Koh Samui with my foot firmly planted on the social accelerator.

Our first test was against Papua New Guinea. The Papua New Guinean players were like balls of gristle, little midget tree stumps. They were incredibly quick and had a strange passion for grabbing their opposing players' clusters — every time one of us made a tackle they would try to peel one of our nuts off. That was a shock to the system, but not as bad as the stories Ridgey had about going over there to play. Apparently, it's real jungle rules there — they were even known to throw poisonous snakes into the changing room at halftime.

The three tests against Papua New Guinea were followed by three tests against England. Back then the song 'Living Next Door to Alice' was big. I was a reserve for the Kiwis in a game in Palmerston North, but apparently the Massey students wanted me on the paddock: the whole of the terraces screamed, 'Ellis, Ellis, where the f--- is Ellis', until Frank put me on. I was so excited by the support, and to be on the field, that as soon as I got there I punched my opponent! It was most unlike me — I don't think I had ever thrown a punch on the field until that day — and the guy was twice the size of me. It was a bloody stupid thing to do. But it was league.

In the final test against England I got named to start the game on the wing, which was great. We were playing in Christchurch and there was a good crowd. With about 20 minutes to go I made a tackle. My knee hit the sprigs of the guy I grabbed, or maybe it was part of the sprinkler system in the ground, and my knee burst. I got up thinking,

'Shit, that hurt', and as I ran back to position I looked down and saw a big lump of mud on my knee. I tried to rub it off, and realised that it wasn't mud; it was a big flap of meat hanging off my shank. I'd cut my leg down to the muscle. I sat down and put my hand up and got carried off on a stretcher. The team doctor gave me some pethidine and soon I was smiling wondrously at everyone. I even helped the nurses clean out the wound before they hooked 30-odd stitches into me.

I ended up having five tests for the Kiwis, and by the end of 1996 I felt like my first year of league had been quite successful. It's been written in the media that I was as proud of playing for the Kiwis as I was for the All Blacks, but that's not true. While it was a thrill to be a Kiwi, the All Blacks felt better for me. For any little boy who grows up in New Zealand playing rugby, being an All Black has to be about as good as it gets.

In 1997 Frank Endacott took over as coach of the Warriors. I ended up solidifying my position on the wing. Frank tried me at centre as well and there was talk of me going to five-eighth, but I didn't think I really understood the game well enough.

At the World Nines in Townsville that year, in the final against Australia, I was coming down the wing, heading for legendary hard man Gorden Tallis. I didn't have a great deal of room to move and it was late in the tackle count, so I decided to chip. I kicked ahead and Gorden launched himself at me. It was late as anything and he hit me chest high and absolutely destroyed me. Glenn Lazarus came over the top and landed on me with a flush elbow and I had to be helped from the field. That was the only time in either code that I was taken out in a tackle. I came back on a few minutes later and we managed to beat the Aussies (and win the World Nines) in their own back yard.

Generally, I've been very lucky with injuries. I had a bad time in 1994, but that was about it. I had one operation on my knee towards the end of my sporting career and my knees don't have the same bounce now: if I go and play a game of touch with my mates I can't jog for the next two days. When I'm older I'm sure it will be worse, but them's the breaks. You can't take all those knocks for all those years and not feel the effects.

At the Super League World Club Challenge in England I slipped over while running the ball back, and a Pommie prop dropped a knee into my face. They were filthy like that, the English, they'd have a go every opportunity they could get. I got up to play the ball and felt my nose sitting on my right cheek. At halftime I went into the changing room and took a look at the damage. It was horrendous. My nose was literally underneath one eye. Frank Endacott caught me looking in the mirror and said, 'Marc, for Christ's sake, you've got a nose like mine now, get back out there and concentrate'. Frank had a nose like a fist and here he was telling me not to worry about it!

In the second half, every time the opposition caught me with the ball they grabbed my nose or leaned on it. Naturally, I tried not to get too involved and, from memory, on one occasion when the ball was kicked to me I kicked it straight back.

That night the local doctor said I'd have to wait six weeks to have my nose reset. That didn't make any sense to me and there was no way I was going to live with a wonky nose, so I went back to my hotel room intent on fixing it myself. In the bathroom I knocked over a few bottles of whisky from the mini-bar, then grabbed it and wrenched it as hard as I could back into its proper place. It made this horrible graunching noise and it bled everywhere, but eventually I got it back where it should have been. When I finished I had two black eyes and a swollen nose, but a straight one. The pain was intense, but nothing compared to the pain of walking around with a crooked beak.

When the next game rolled around about a week later, my nose was still fairly fragile. I knew that the Poms knew that I'd broken my nose, and judging by the last game I knew they'd do everything they could to break it again, so I pulled a hamstring in training and sat the next game out. It was the only time I ever did that. I wasn't one of those players who could say, 'Oh well, it's a battle scar'. I knew that if it broke again, not only would I not be able to breathe out of it, but I'd likely never have a girlfriend again, so I blew the game off.

People say league is tougher than union, but I think it's about the same. In league you don't get stuck at the bottom of a ruck and get kicked and rucked and stood on like you do in union. But in union you seldom get king-hit by a couple of guys every time you run the ball back. You can get on the end of some massive shots in league and a lot of the players are built to tackle.

League was a very different environment to union. It was very individualistic. Other than training there wasn't a collective way the team prepared for each game — the guys did as they wished. In union, you'd get on a bus on the way to an Otago or All Blacks game and, as I have already mentioned, there would be absolute silence. I had a very methodical way of going about my day before a game. In league you weren't in camp the night before if you had a home game. In the changing room before a game players put music on and they'd all be laughing and cracking up. That's the way they'd been doing it for years, and I found it quite liberating, but it was a bit of a culture shock to be in an environment that was so flexible, and I think possibly it was a weakness for the team.

Socially, it was an odd environment too. We all got on famously and there was a laidback camaraderie, but after the game most people would just push off and go home. I missed the after-match and having a few with the boys, sitting down and dissecting the game and having a few laughs. At the end of each season we'd have a Mad Monday, where the team would go to a pub and have a few beers together. Everyone loved that experience so why that didn't happen on a more regular basis I'm not sure. I think it's probably the pressure of people having families and it being a professional game. It felt very much like a job.

The Warriors supporters were fantastic. They were such passionate people and they were real grassroots New Zealanders. What you see is what you get with them and I like that in people, so I got on really well with the supporters at the Warriors. I guess there were a few true-blue league supporters who thought, 'Ah, he's a bloody rugby union player', but most of them were incredibly supportive of me. When we didn't get the results, though, some supporters felt disillusioned with us. The public started searching for reasons why they weren't getting the wins they were promised, and the media started looking for scapegoats.

That led to a lot of criticism that Ridgey and I should concentrate on league and shouldn't do any TV stuff. People thought that it was detracting from our ability to play the game, but that was absolute bloody nonsense. Filming took up only an afternoon a week, and we did it after training. If we had been doing something traditional, like working as an electrician or a plumber, there would have been no problem in the world. Anyway, I think it's really important to have something outside of the sport. I think you can become quite insular and quite focused on sport and sport alone if you don't.

There were signs at the end of 1997 that I was on the outer a wee bit. The Warriors hadn't had a great year — we'd missed out on the Super League play-offs and lost to Brisbane in the semi-finals of the World Club Challenge — but Frank had picked me for the Kiwis the year before, and I'd been touted as a player to watch the following season, so I couldn't quite get my head around that.

In 1998 it came to my attention that the management thought I was being paid too much. We'd had a couple of average years and the crowds were shrinking, and there were obviously serious financial concerns for the Warriors, so the management had taken a second look at some of the bigger contracts they'd signed. The Warriors wanted to halve my contract. Not surprisingly, I said no. I wanted them to honour the contract they'd given me. It was intimated that if I didn't agree to the revised contract I'd be stuck in the second grade.

'That's cool', I said, 'I really enjoy playing second grade'. That wasn't the response that the Warriors thought they'd be getting, but it was true. Playing second grade for the Warriors was a good time. The guys were honest players, either on their way up or in the grade for good; hard buggers but keen for a laugh and playing for all the right reasons. Some of the jokes they cracked on the field had me rolling and the thrill they got from representing their province or club reminded me of the Otago days. And, although it wasn't as physically challenging as the top stuff, playing second division meant I didn't have to go to Aussie every second weekend.

It was also frustrating at times. And it wasn't how I had wanted to finish my league career. When I first started playing rugby for Otago, my dad said to me, 'Keep your head about yourself because one day there will be tough times'. That's the same with 99 per cent of all sporting careers and, sure enough, with the Warriors, it happened. The media jumped on my relegation and said I was playing poorly.

The moment you start listening to the press, whether they're raving about you or bagging you, you're on a road to disaster. The media is based around sensationalism because that's what sells, so if something's average they'll call it bad, and if something's good they'll call it brilliant. You have to take it all with a grain of salt. I've seen so many examples of people riding a wave, believing the hype, and when it's come crashing down they've had a long way to fall. One of the big challenges when life is quite cushy is to remember to keep your feet on the ground. I've learnt to enjoy the wave, but to expect it to come back down again, as it did in 1998.

The whole contract scenario became quite undignified and personal and it led to me becoming increasingly fed up and disillusioned with league. I was frustrated that my sporting career was coming to an end playing second grade and arguing over dollars. I was worried that I would come out of league and people would say my career had been a failure. I lost a degree of confidence and once your confidence goes at that top level, it's very difficult.

People love to say that professional rugby players and league players are paid too much. They don't understand the pressure that we are playing under, and the responsibility. The best I can liken it to is this: imagine you had to stand up in front of quarter of a million people every Saturday and make a speech. If the audience likes your speech you get a pat on the back, but if they don't, every one of those people, including all the media, thinks that you are shit and tells you so. That's the sort of pressure you're under every week playing sport at that level. (I don't reckon an All Black's salary is a huge amount of money for that.) They're paid well, but you've got to be very thick-skinned and able to take consistent knocks, all the while continuing to believe in yourself. That's where Laurie's 'dump it and move on' philosophy helps.

The chances of having a long career in professional sport are slim. You can have a form slump; others come up through the ranks and replace you; injury can end your career in a moment; and politics comes into play. There will always be dozens of intangibles that are completely out of your control that can come between you and a living. It's not the kind of money you can live off for the rest of your life anyway (unless you're a one-off like Jonah Lomu). Even amazing players like Christian Cullen have to go and play overseas to make sufficient money to settle down.

I tell young kids who tell me they want to be rugby players to go for it, but to concentrate on their schoolwork first and foremost. Schoolwork is the most important thing because you need that back-up plan — the chance of having a professional sporting career, no matter how talented you are, has to be one in 10,000. There are so many things that could work against you and it's highly unlikely you're going to earn enough money in rugby to live off for the rest of your life, so you need an alternative.

I was very lucky that I moved from rugby to business in a relatively seamless way. A lot of our young players come out of sport with no training to do anything else. Their families haven't encouraged them to have an alternative, but they've got used to the new, expensive lifestyle. No one's told them to create a back-up plan, because managers and agents don't make any money out of back-up plans.

I read once that in American football 75 per cent of players come out of the sport bankrupt, divorced or both. I can believe it. The players themselves have to take some of the blame. I saw a classic example of this at the Warriors. One year KPMG, one of the Warriors' sponsors, offered to come and give free financial advice to the players in the form of a seminar. I had a financial advisor, and my money was working for me, but I decided to go along, and I was one of only eight in the team who signed up for it. When the day of the seminar rolled around only three of us turned up — the others had decided at the last minute to go and play a round of golf. That's why players end up with no prospects and a couple of hundred thousand dollars to live off for the rest of their lives. A lot of people will say that's a challenge they'd be happy to have, but it's pretty daunting if you don't have the skills to manage your money.

American studies have shown that the mental effects of becoming unemployed are similar to finding out you have a terminal illness.

I can believe that too. At 30, retiring players don't have the life skills of a 65-year-old preparing himself for retirement. Often these players have a wife and kids who have experienced life in the fast lane. When this grinds to a halt it can be an incredibly daunting time for a young man.

I had a 'three-year plus two' contract with the Warriors. That meant that I could sign up for another two years with the Warriors once my contract was completed, at my discretion. When the Warriors shafted me into the second grade, I said, 'By the way, I give you notice that I'll exercise my right to have another two years with the club, at the same amount you've been paying me'. That freaked them out so the management offered to buy me out of my contract. I took them up on that and started discussions with the North Harbour Rugby Union.

I had said I'd never play against my old Otago team-mates, but by then times had changed; the personnel had changed. Most of my mates had moved on. Anton Oliver, Tony Brown and Taine Randell were the only three players from my day still in the team.

North Harbour offered me my first taste of professional rugby, albeit at NPC level. Buck Shelford was a guy I'd played against when I first started playing rugby and now he was my coach. I thought the North Harbour culture was similar to the Otago culture and would probably be good for me. Both sides had the ability to play brilliantly and the ability to have a bad day, and it was never a conformist environment. The rugby promised to be similar to the free-spirited game that we played in Otago. There was a great team culture and we had some good fellas in that team. And the North Harbour players used to enjoy a bit of high-spirited mischief.

My confidence, though, wasn't what it was when I played for Otago, and the whole process of being relegated by the Warriors had knocked me. When I started playing rugby, I always expected myself to be the guy who scored the winning try. Almost 10 years later, at the end of my sporting career, I had become the guy who hoped he wouldn't miss that important tackle. It was a small shift inside my head, but it was massive in terms of my demeanour, my thought process and my ability to attack.

I really enjoyed that first season in spite of that, even though it was mediocre in terms of results. I enjoyed jumping on the wing and having a run around. It was great to be playing rugby again and to have something I could sink my teeth into. Towards the end of the season Frank Bunce opted out and I managed to get into centre, where I stayed for the next couple of seasons.

The following year I got picked for the Blues in the Super 12, which was interesting. Our first game was against Otago at Carisbrook. Here I was, the guy who had been promoting the hell out of the Otago way of life every opportunity I got, now playing against Otago. I got a fairly tepid reception. There were a few students on the sideline giving me what for, and they got even more vocal when, on the wing, I came in and put a head-high tackle on Taine Randell!

The Blues had a new coach, Jed Rowlands, and he found that season very tough. It seemed like he didn't have any understanding of what was required in terms of a game plan at that level and the season started to go horribly downhill. We played some pretty poor rugby. There were all sorts of selection challenges and changes and I was on the wing for only half the season, then replaced by Doug Howlett. I think Jed probably made the right decision putting Dougie in. He was a lot younger than me, a lot hungrier, and a lot better looking. And he's gone on to prove he's a better winger than I was.

By the middle of the season Jed was battling with how to get the guys back on track. In the Otago days Gordy had occasionally pulled out a mid-week court session. We would turn up to training on a Tuesday and expect to get flogged and instead there'd be a couple of kegs of beer. We'd sit around and have a few drinks together, and leave having had a bit of a blow-out, and feeling like we'd let the turkey timer out a wee bit and eased the pressure. I suggested this to Jed and, sure enough, the next week we turned up for training and he said, 'OK fellas, we've got a keg on. You can stay and have a few beers or you can go home early.'

In Otago that would have been met with rapturous applause. Everyone would have sat down and got merrily inebriated. That day in the Blues changing room three of us stayed. We would have had to drink about 15 litres of beer each to get through it all! That, in a way, summarised the difference between Otago rugby and Auckland rugby. And amateurism and professionalism.

By 1999 my heart wasn't really in it any more. I had lost my passion for rugby, and I was getting bored with the mental aspect of the game. With rugby there's always the same mental process of having to peak for the game. The physical condition wasn't a problem, but I had tired of the mental process.

That changed when I moved back to Dunedin to play in the Super 12 for the Highlanders in 2000. I got back to grassroots rugby and to a place that I knew. The culture had changed thanks to professionalism, but the same ethos ran underneath it all, the same history and traditions and values that I'd enjoyed years ago. They were still quite old school, Otago. Maybe that was because of guys like Anton Oliver, who had been there and seen the old-school traditions that had been passed down and had carried them on.

I knew I'd be received with open arms down south and that was a good feeling. I moved in with Josh Kronfeld out at St Clair Beach and got selected at fullback/wing and started in every game. We got beaten in the semi-finals by the Crusaders, but it was great to get back into that old familiar environment, get back into the changing room that I remembered so well, and back to the whole Otago culture. I hadn't really grown out of the student lifestyle (and to this day I'm not sure that I have, which is possibly a bit sad because I'm now 35 and the people at varsity are half my age). I found it hellishly refreshing and the upshot was that I didn't have to try so hard to play well again. It felt natural again. I had a lovely four or five months there.

My final NPC season I was back at North Harbour. I wanted to play that last season so I could say I had a decade playing top-level sport. If I'd bailed out a year earlier I would have regretted it I think, but in the end I'd had enough.

My very last game I actually started off on the bench, but I really didn't care at that stage. I'd ended up playing 24 games for North Harbour, and it was cool to just get to the end of the game, say goodbye to the guys in the team, and leave. It was time to move on. I was ready for a new challenge.

The Juice, the Whole Juice, and Nothing but the Juice

In 1999, as my rugby career was coming to an end, my best mate Simon Neal and I decided to set up a juice company. It wasn't my first commercial experience; the year before I had invested in Leftfield, a huge bar development down at the Auckland Viaduct.

Leftfield was the brainchild of Kevin Roberts, Geoff Vuleta and Ric Salizzo. I had first met Kevin when I made the All Blacks and he was running Lion Nathan. Steinlager was an All Blacks sponsor and back then Kevin was hot on the idea of a study grant for the students in the team. Of course, I hounded him constantly about that and in my last year in the All Blacks got one.

Leftfield was to have a massive stand for 150 people and a big screen to watch games on. 'Sports Café' was to be filmed there every Wednesday night. It was a fantastic idea, the biggest bar in New Zealand. The more I listened the greater the potential seemed and all the research indicated that it would be a success, so I invested in it. Leftfield went superbly well for a while; all the initial signs were fantastic. After the All Blacks played Australia at Eden Park in 1999 it turned over something like $140,000 in one evening, to this day one of the biggest days in the history of New Zealand bars. But it was a costly, big machine and there were huge overheads: rent, and staff. The food was fairly ordinary and nobody took the dining potential seriously. We went through several bar managers and they all had ideas about bringing in clientele, but nothing really worked.

Looking back on it, some big mistakes were made. The bar was on the wrong side of the wharf, so there was limited sun and it was quite windy. On the other side where there was afternoon sun would have been a better proposition I think, because people like to have a beer in the sun looking out at the water (although it would have affected the big screen). None of the investors had time to devote to the bar once it started floundering, and once the speed wobbles kicked in, it was game over really. Ric was left steering the ship a wee bit because he was an investor and he was working out of there, and I felt really sorry for him. I lost my investment, which wasn't insignificant. Certainly some of the big boys went longer, but it was enough for me to hurt.

The failings of Leftfield taught me some valuable lessons, and I am the kind of bloke who learns best from experience. The biggest thing I learnt was that one should look closely before investing in something. If you're not hands-on, if you don't have control, it's a lot harder to protect your investment. Also, I went in on it based on the other people involved. In hindsight, while they had all been successful in other business ventures, our collective experience in running a bar was limited. I should have thought of that.

Neither Simon nor I had ever run a juice company before we set up shop, but we both knew about good-quality juice. Richard Hoggard, one of our best mates from school, had a business (along with his brother Tom) in Wellington called the Daily Squeeze. The Daily Squeeze was exactly as the name suggests: the boys would bring in fresh oranges from Gisborne and squeeze them in their factory and supply local bars and restaurants with the juice. We used to go down every now and then to help out and do a bit of squeezing and have a laugh. It was quite a cool little operation on Blair Street, right off Courtenay Place. (Naturally, helping out on a Friday night afforded the best views in town as the bars filled up with ladies.)

Simon and I decided that we could do something similar in Auckland, in a little space down at the Viaduct. We rented a space and put a concrete floor down, invested about $10,000 each, spent $3000 on a machine, and called our company The Daily O. Simon would get down there early in the morning, about 5.30 a.m., squeeze for a few hours, then start deliveries. I'd pop in before and after training at North Harbour.

At that time the Viaduct was under construction, so we targeted all the cafés that were already set up with a one-page presentation that showed the cost of the product and the differences between our juice and everyone else's. It wasn't the toughest sales job in the world, but we discovered that the market was quite price-sensitive. Despite the fact that we had the best-tasting juice (that was 100 per cent freshly squeezed), made-from-concentrate products like Le Jus sold for less. Our raw material costs were so much higher and retailers could taste the difference, but they didn't want to pay more for it, or to pass that cost on to the consumer. In our presentation we suggested to café owners that the consumer would not mind paying $3.50 per glass for the real thing, as opposed to $3 for juice made from concentrate. Some of them saw the logic in this; some of them didn't. So we had to shrink our margins and sell our juice for $3.50 per litre rather than $5. We had such small overheads that that wasn't really a problem and it was a good lesson to learn.

Not long after Simon and I got the business up and running, I got a phone call from Stefan Lepionka. Back in the days of the Daily Squeeze, when we were in Wellington, Stefan was the other guy in Wellington making fresh juice. He'd started his operation — Stefan's — when he was 16 and built it into a big successful business (but he was from St Pat's, and we were from Wellington College, so we were rooting for our mates at the Daily Squeeze).

Stefan was born with an eye for a dollar. He and I first met when we were about 12. He and his mate Stacey Jackson procured the rights to the ice-cream cart at the Basin Reserve. This was in the early 1980s when the Basin Reserve was really humming. It had a fantastic atmosphere and I loved to go there for the cricket, loved watching Jeremy Coney and Bruce Edgar on the pitch. Dad would come with me; he'd drop me off at the terraces and go and sit in the Members' stand, and every now and then he'd come and check on me.

The terraces were a hell of a lot of fun. When a member came down to the terrace, the crowd used to chant, 'Take your tie off' until they did. If a stunner came past, or even a roughie later in the day, the chant would go up for them to take something else off. (A girl had to be dog-tucker not to get a chant after 3 p.m., once the refreshments had taken their toll.) This made the more modest of girls walk along the top of the bank rather than around the front.

Guys used to sneak in the night before, dig a big hole, and bury a keg where they'd be planning to sit the next day. They'd rock up the next day with the keg hose, stick an umbrella up, and be sorted with 50 litres of chilled beer, at the right price and with no queues!

Each day Stefan and Stacey would load up their cart with Ice Chocs and Joy Bars and go around the Basin hawking their wares. I watched what they were doing: they were giving as many ice creams away as they were selling, but they were still making money hand over fist, so I went up to them and said, 'Any chance of a job on your ice-cream cart?'. 'Nah,' they said. I wasn't very happy with that, so I made a plan. Their cart was a three-wheeler thing and if they got enough speed up from under the R A Vance stand (where they restocked), they could get halfway around the ground with one of them sitting on the front and one on the back pedalling like hell. I waited until they got a running roll with a laden cart one day and as they came past me I stuck my cricket bat under the wheels. The whole cart went out of control; there were ice creams everywhere. All the little kids ran in and grabbed them off the ground. It was pretty tense for a minute, but the boys decided it was better to have me with them than against them and they gave me a job.

It was a brilliant set-up. I got to get into the Basin Reserve for free, and on top of that I was paid $20 to work the cart. I made another $50 a day by jumping the fence, selling ground passes to people waiting outside, then jumping back in. And I was giving away as many ice creams as I could to my mates, which made me fairly popular.

Stefan, Stacey and I used to love to rark up the crowd. We'd hold the Aussie flag up when New Zealand was playing Australia and the crowd would pelt us with beer cans. This was back in the days of the steel beer can (you could throw that further than the aluminium one that followed — now it's the plastic cup, which you can't really throw at all, which is disappointing to some). Nine out of every 10 cans thrown was empty, but occasionally a smart-arse threw a full one. During an Aussie vs. New Zealand one-dayer I got a full can in the shin and I remember the pain to this day. We escaped by diving over the fence into the field of play. They had to stop the game while we were escorted back over the fence to the cart and all the cans had to be swept off the field. I think that incident was the first time I ever appeared on TV.

Later that same day Greg Matthews, the Aussie cricketer everyone loved to hate, got a toilet seat thrown at him. He was fielding right down in front of the terraces and someone did a Beatrice Faumuina discus with a toilet seat. It just missed him and had the Aussie team up in arms for the remainder of the tour.

Another incident I recall from the Basin was when a guy was walking past the terraces, wearing a steel army helmet, inciting the crowd with the fingers and the odd salute (he must have been Australian). The crowd started to shower him with cans of beer. He head-butted a few, which just incensed the crowd further, and when he got about two-thirds of the way around the terraces a guy sitting in the first tier, at ground level, threw a full can underarm, up under his helmet. The can hit him flush on his nose. Helmet-head hit the deck, his nose exploded, and the whole place cracked up with glee.

The Basin was my first taste of streaking. There was always a streaker or two entertaining the terraces. It was good, clean fun. While at university I ventured back for a one-dayer at the Basin for the cricket and a mate volunteered to do a streak from the terraces, across the pitch, if we paid him $50. We raised about $20 among the fellas, but needed more, so we widened the net and made an announcement to those seated around us. We got $50 quick smart. He dashed through the pitch in the nude with a backpack on his back (followed the whole way by the TV cameras), jumped the fence, and disappeared up towards Newtown. Half an hour later he came back with a few pizzas and beer for all the boys with his winnings!

I did the cart with Stefan and Stacey for a couple of summers. If I was making $70 a day, those guys were making at least $150 each. They used to go home at night on the bus to Seatoun and count their money out along the back seat.

Simon and I were stoked to hear from Stefan almost 20 years later. He was just back from London, where he'd been working in the juice industry, and was looking for something to do. It made sense to get him on board given his experience. We had a meeting or two with him and he eventually told Simon and me that it was impossible for us to make a living the way we were going, but that he had some ideas, ways we could improve things.

Stefan Lepionka, co-founder and CEO of Charlie's: I told them that it was too hard, not a good business opportunity. People didn't want to pay a premium price for the juice. But I could see the power Marc would have in building the brand. He was a personality and he was not only a television presenter, but he was also the face of Fresh Up. This was an opportunity for him to build his own brand. I said I might be interested in it if I could be a silent partner.

Stefan called on a couple of contacts from his Wellington days to get fruit in for a cheaper price. We started getting it delivered by the pallet from Gisborne. We extended our control of the Viaduct's juice supply, then looked to the cafés and restaurants on Ponsonby Road.

We started mocking up labels and looks for The Daily O, but we quickly realised it was fairly restrictive as a name. While The Daily O told the story, it had zero personality. We decided a change was in order, so the three of us sat down at Leftfield one day and over a beer we came up with Charlie's. We wanted to call it something that people would have an affinity with, something a bit cheeky and irreverent we could use to create a more tangible relationship with the customer. We wanted a name that differentiated it from every other juice on the market, and one we could use if, one day, we wanted to go into bread or milk or some other product. Charlie's sounds quite old school and quite classic and we felt comfortable with it immediately. Branding had been one of those varsity subjects that I'd been really interested in and I knew we could have a bit of fun with Charlie's — everyone's been a bit of a Charlie at some stage in their life.

One of the first marketing ploys we came up with was to employ Charlie's Angels, young women to sell the juice. We'd hire mates of mates or girls we saw on the street who looked right for the job. They'd walk around in these snug Charlie's T-shirts, with a tool belt full of juice bottles, selling them to all the builders working at the Viaduct. I don't think those builders had ever been so healthy; they gave up fizzy drinks and waited like Pavlov's dogs for the girls to come by every afternoon.

At that stage the biggest juice brands in New Zealand were Just Juice and Fresh Up, both owned by Frucor. Fresh Up was the sponsor of 'Fresh Up In The Deep End', one of the shows Ridgey and I were doing, and we fronted their TV ads. Before long I got a letter from Frucor asking if I was involved in Charlie's. They had caught wind of it because their reps had gone into some of the cafés where our juice had replaced theirs. I told Frucor I was not hands on, that I was a pretty silent partner.

It was a bit of a fib, but not entirely, as I was limited as to what I could do for Charlie's while I was still playing for North Harbour. I respected their request that I not front Charlie's, and I could understand and appreciate their concerns. And I knew come the end of the year Frucor wouldn't renew my contract. That was a significant contract to lose, but it was an opportunity cost I was prepared to live with because I believed in Charlie's.

When Stefan joined us, our relationship with Frucor became even more tricky, because Frucor had bought Stefan's business from him in 1994. In its prime Stefan's had 75 per cent market share in supermarket chilled juice. It and Simply Squeezed were the two biggest products in the chiller. Frucor went nationwide with Stefan's and to save costs switched from a not-from-concentrate product to a reconstituted product (juice concentrate and added water) like all the others on the market. It wanted to create a consistent product (squeezed juice can taste different from week to week because of the fruit) and to drive down costs and deliver a better margin.

Stefan Lepionka: That ended acrimoniously. Frucor bought into the business and promised a huge amount for it and me personally. I was to stay with the brand. I thought I would be there forever, but as soon as we signed the deal, they tried to oust me. They spent three years making it unbearable for me. I'm a stubborn prick, but in the end I went. Of course, now the Stefan's brand is no longer around. They destroyed it. They thought they were smarter than the consumer and they changed Stefan's recipe.

Stefan learnt from that and it gave him some real savvy; and he and the management of Frucor have been competitive ever since. There's no love lost between them. When Mark Cowsill, Frucor's managing director, caught wind that we were all working together, he met with Stefan, and asked what we were doing. After hearing Stefan out, Cowsill suggested Stefan get back into his overalls and squeeze some fruit. His point, I guess, was to remind Stefan that he was starting at the bottom again. We knew then Charlie's was on the radar and we were starting to get up his nose.

Soon after Stefan became a partner in Charlie's a couple of Greek guys from Melbourne contacted him with a deal. They had these machines that would squeeze the oranges for us. Stefan and Simon went over to Melbourne to check them out. They got absolutely wined and dined — it was all turned on for them. The machines were innovative and we started to think that if we got them into key supermarkets around New Zealand we could give New Zealand a taste of real, fresh juice on a regular basis.

I met with Hugh Perret, then the managing director of Foodstuffs (which owns New World and Pak 'N Save), and he gave us our first break really, a deal to put the fresh juice machines in 30 supermarkets around the country. So in November 1999 we put our first machine into the New World at Victoria Park in Auckland.

It went gangbusters. We did some massive numbers — on our best week there we sold about 4000 litres, which was extraordinary. We put our next machine into Wellington City New World and then moved on down the country all the way to Wakatipu. Each machine cost us around $20,000, so by the time we'd bought 30 machines and slowly rolled them out it was a big punt.

Stefan and I set off on our first marketing campaign, a nationwide tour of supermarkets (while Simon held the fort in Auckland). We'd go to each supermarket, talk about the product to shoppers, and give it away. That's a pretty time-consuming and knackering process, but it's the best way to sell juice. We knew that when we said to New Zealanders, 'Try this product, it's going to be good', that we were telling the truth, and could deliver on all our promises. And we knew that we needed to create a real public interest in the product if consumers were going to come through the door and ask for it by name.

The three of us fell into our roles at Charlie's and we did it in a really easy way. We had a flat structure. Stefan was our CEO: he had experience and knew what the potential was and saw the big picture really well. Simon was really capable in terms of logistics. And I reckon I was alright at making sure the brand meant what it should. We had lively debate, but we always ended up agreeing on decisions. There were never any blow-ups in the office.

It was a fun time. I think the early days of setting up a company are the most enjoyable because you see an enormous number of things happen in a short space of time. Yet you have enough time to sit down and enjoy it as you go.

We had some cracker moments. We went to Melbourne to meet Gino Vescio, the general manager of the Original Juice Company, and had a very eventful trip. The night before we were to meet him, Stefan and I went out and had a few drinks. On the way home Stefan was having a leak (I was sitting on a park bench waiting for him, minding my own business) when three guys leapt out of a car and, totally unprovoked, started attacking him. I went over and tried to break it up, but these guys were rough buggers. One of them hit me and my immediate reaction was to hit him back. Then he pulled a knife on me and Stefan and I realised we were really out of our depth.

We took off sprinting down the road, dressed in our suits and ties, but I slipped over in my leather-soled shoes. The guy caught up to me and stabbed me in the back of the head while the others dragged Stefan off. I bolted, jumped into a nearby taxi van, and told the driver to put his foot on it. As soon as he saw the guys who were chasing me he grabbed the keys, jumped out and ran off yelling, 'Run for your life!'.

It was a nightmare: I tried to lock myself in the cab, but they got the door open and started bashing me around the legs with metal pipes. I was getting peppered on the legs and arms, so I tried to attack. That didn't work; I got biffed in the nose with a pipe. Eventually, I got free and ran into a nearby nightclub and the bouncers kept my attackers out. A nice young lady, a nurse, drove me to the hospital. I ended up with seven stitches in the back of my head and 35 in my nose, after some plastic surgery.

I had lost Stefan and was so worried I went around every hospital in Melbourne. When I didn't find him I became convinced that he was dead. I got back to the hotel in a very sorry state, only to find him tucked up in bed snoring, with just a tiny nick on his nose.

It was a scary experience and, in a strange way, a defining moment in our relationship. Stefan knew from then on that he had someone watching his back at all costs. And I did too. I already knew that about Simon, and that, I think, is one of the greatest strengths that we had as a company: the three guys who founded it are all intensely loyal to one another. That continues today. We'd never shit on each other. And that, in business, is fairly unique.

The next day we went to see Gino. Stefan knew Gino — they'd both been in the juice business a long time — and Stefan had some great stories about him. Apparently, the big fruit growers in Australia are seen to be a bit like the Mafia, in that they have a stronghold on the industry, which can be a bit intimidating.

We rolled into Gino's house and it was just like Tony's house on 'The Sopranos'. It was set up on a hill with all-day sun, a swimming pool, and a tennis court. Gino came out. He was the most splendidly turned-out chap I'd ever seen. He had the beautiful suit, the stylish hair, the olive skin — and here was I with 30 stitches in my face. We had a beautiful dinner, played a bit of snooker. We had balloons of cognac and smoked cigars. It was a cool experience, and to this day we still do a lot of business with Gino in Melbourne. He's one of the industry's real characters.

One day we met with a local New Zealand supermarket owner who had one of our machines in his store. We told him what location we thought the machine would be best in and he took that as a real affront, that we were telling him what to do. He refused to deal with us from then on. There have been one or two meetings like that, where we've pushed too hard, just because we've been so keen. We were so passionate about Charlie's, so driven, that often it was perceived as being a bit too aggressive.

We made the same mistake when we first went to Gisborne to see the orange growers. They all turned up looking very much like growers, and we showed up in suits and ties. We had a PowerPoint presentation prepared and everything and they thought we were real Auckland wankers. It took a couple of years of good business results to get those growers on-side. We should have realised they'd be old school. The best thing we could have done with those guys is to have had a chat over a beer.

In some meetings you could cut the air with a knife as soon as we walked in. Ninety per cent of people have been really keen to help, really keen to see us succeed, but there were 10 per cent who were waiting to crush us. I learnt that some people want to make it hard for you to succeed sometimes — they don't want to make it too easy for a small company.

I try to never be overawed by a situation or an opportunity or a person. What's the worst that could happen?, I ask myself. If you ask a girl out, she could say no. If you pitch an idea to someone, they might not like it. That's not the worst thing that could happen. The worst thing is that you didn't give it a crack in the first place. When I go into meetings with big swinging dicks I think of a line from Bob Marley in his song 'Coming In From the Cold': 'The biggest man you ever did see was just a baby.'

A year after introducing the juice machines we realised they had limited scope. They were cool and innovative, but managing them in-store was a big challenge.

Stefan Lepionka: It was tough on a day-in, day-out basis. Each machine was like a factory, so it was like running 30 factories in New Zealand. It didn't work because the juice was still expensive and we were targeting a very small part of the market. But we had built a brand through the process. That was how people knew there was a fresh-juice brand called Charlie's. We had a brand to go and do something with. Because of Marc's personality, he was telling everyone he met about Charlie's. We were getting people calling all the time wanting to know why they couldn't get the juice. We couldn't put 12,000 machines out there — it was too hard — so we decided to package it so it was available nationwide.

We brought in packaged goods — a one-litre tetra pak, and bottles for the chiller. They had to be made in Australia because we wanted to make large volumes and keep the juice unadulterated. There wasn't enough fruit in New Zealand for us to make our pure juice — we'd have used the entire New Zealand juice crop in about 12 weeks — so we went to Mildura in Victoria, Australia, to have it picked, squeezed and packaged.

Our competitors, Rio and Frucor, owned the only juice packaging facility in New Zealand that could do tetra paks, so there was no chance of them packing our product. If we had a packaging agreement with them, they would have known our costs, lines of supply, volumes, and so on. (To be fair, however, that sort of info is easy enough to come by.)

As we introduced Charlie's tetra paks we phased the machines out. The finished product was shipped over in massive quantities to New Zealand, and we put our money where our mouth was with an advertising campaign. Progressive Enterprises' supermarkets wouldn't quite commit to selling the tetra packs, so we had to go nationwide with an advertising campaign and create demand without knowing if Progressive would come onboard.

Stefan Lepionka: We took a huge personal risk. Hundreds and hundreds of thousands of dollars were being poured into the business until we got traction.

That was a bloody big gamble, but without the ad campaign we weren't going to get anywhere. We had to back ourselves and spend the money and trust our gut feel was accurate. We had the product sitting there in a warehouse — sufficient volume that if Progressive said yes, we had the product. Fortunately, it happened as we predicted. And we literally went from nothing to number one in three months.

Stefan Lepionka: We all agreed that to be in this industry you have to think big. This business is all about brand and distribution. We believed in the idea and in each other, so we needed to use our individual skills to build our business. We'd got ourselves a brand; we just had to organise distribution.

I took Stefan to see Peter Kean, managing director of Lion Nathan, about a distribution deal. I'd known Keano for years, since I was in the Otago team. It was a key break — we got distribution and credibility within the industry. We were able to tap in to the Lion Nathan machine: that meant using its key account relationships, promotional strategies, and reps and merchandisers. And it was a huge sign of faith in our brand.

Stefan Lepionka: Lion Nathan helped launch the Charlie's brand into the marketplace. They gave us the credibility that was required at that time. It was a huge turning point for us, *the* turning point. If it weren't for Marc, it never would have happened. Marc was the door opener. He got our story across. And the tetra orange became the largest-selling one-litre tetra in New Zealand supermarkets, by sales, bigger than Fresh Up, and that's because of Lion Nathan's distribution.

That break, and then the juice selling so bloody well, signalled our arrival in the juice market.

At varsity I once had to do a mock interview as part of one of my marketing courses. The interviewer asked how being an All Black would help me in a marketing career. I hated talking about being an All Black. It made me uncomfortable. It was part of my life, a chapter, but I didn't want it to be seen as defining me. I wanted people to see me for who I really was, so I gave him a stock standard response: I'm pretty good at dealing with pressure, good in a team environment, dealing with the media, blah, blah, blah. Then I said that New Zealand was a small country and I'd met some pretty influential people, and that who you knew counted for something in business.

I walked out of that interview thinking I'd aced it, and I hadn't. I hadn't done very well at all. The lecturer said that by saying it's who you know I'd intimidate people, and he marked me down for it. That's the most ludicrous thing anyone's ever said to me. And it showed the lecturer's ignorance a wee bit. If I didn't know my mate Keano at Lion I would never have been able to run the distribution idea past him. Sure, the proposition had legs, but I stand by the notion that it's who you know sometimes. The more contacts you've got, the better you can do. (That's also why you should never treat anyone like shit on the ascent, as it will be remembered on the descent.)

Once the products and their distribution were in place, we got into the game of creating a brand. That's the part that I found really exciting. We'd had a few good wins and the business was growing. The office environment was a bit loose and a lot of fun. We got a huge thrill out of seeing our products on the shelf. We loved seeing the ads on TV, calling round our friends and getting feedback on them.

We started selling first-grade whole fruit, so we could offer the growers a market for the whole tree, basically. We bought the grade one, two and three oranges and mandarins, exported some, sold some as fruit in the produce department, and juiced the rest. That's been fantastic. People go into the supermarket, see the fruit, and are reminded that we sell Charlie's juice.

As we grew the business we had to understand what the forecasts were, what sort of potential upside there could be from the advertising campaigns, and what product we would need to have on hand if we got another supermarket chain onboard. There were always so many intangibles to consider and Simon and Stefan had to be as accurate as possible with that educated guesswork. I was the marketing manager. I'd never had any commercial experience in marketing, I hadn't spent the last 10 years in the marketing department of a big corporate, but I was passionate about our brand. When we started I never thought of Charlie's being a career for me. It was more a sideline while I was playing a bit of sport, a project that Simon would run. But as time went on, I realised it was a goer, and we grew rapidly, and my strengths were in understanding where the brand should be positioned and how best to deliver the message that our juice was not like the others.

Juice Wars, 'Cheeky Darkies', and Other Controversies

The hundreds of hours Charlie's has spent trying to get the likes of Simply Squeezed, Just Juice, Fresh Up, McCoy's and Arano to change their messages to consumers is a story in itself.

The big players use reconstituted juice most, if not all, of the time to reduce costs (and create a consistent flavour year round). The juice is 'reconstituted' from concentrate, which you can buy from all over the world. You just add water. Most New Zealanders don't know what 'reconstituted' means. If the juice companies put 'concentrate and tap water' on the label, buyers would be put off. I personally believe it's an intentional muddying of the waters and it's misleading. For example, Simply Squeezed Orange Juice can have up to nine ingredients in it, but going by the brand name alone you'd assume it's just squeezed orange juice.

Shoppers don't read the back labels on products, and nor should they — there are tens of thousands of products on supermarket shelves and consumers can't be expected to research them all. That's why the Fair Trading Act stipulates that a brand name cannot be misleading or deceptive. By that rationale, I believe Just Juice should just be juice; Fresh Up should be fresh; likewise Simply Squeezed.

Charlie's juice doesn't contain concentrate and we're resolute that we won't ever. It would be so easy for us to slip a few extra ingredients in, to halve our costs and double our profits. But we can't do that (except for vitamin C, which we add back to the juice). We've intentionally painted ourselves into a corner by marketing Charlie's as not from concentrate juice. We want to be honest because people don't expect to get bullshitted by us. They know that there are two guys (me and Stefan) whose pictures are on the side of every pack, and are therefore directly accountable. That's very different to the ivory towers the owners of our bigger competitors are in; you won't see their faces on the side of their juice. But our product means we have a higher raw material cost — about 18 apples go into every one litre of our apple juice. We can't do the deep discounts like other companies can.

Stefan Lepionka: You're always disadvantaged if you make a product without taking shortcuts — it's going to be more expensive. If we added water and sugar we'd be twice as profitable today, but it just didn't sit well with us. If we do that, what's our point of difference with the brand? We had to stick to our beliefs. Of course, the average consumer doesn't wake up thinking about juice; they think about their mortgage, their relationship, getting the kids off to school. A food product is irrelevant. And consumers don't want to buy a more expensive product, so with Charlie's it comes down to education.

We spend most of our marketing dollars, sadly, telling consumers of our point of difference. If the juice industry were correctly regulated, like it is in the United States, United Kingdom and Australia, we wouldn't have to do that. New Zealand's just a joke with regard to beverage labelling, so we try to make sure that the people who are buying anyone else's product know what they're missing out on.

We've been trying to get something done about labelling in the industry since the early days of Charlie's. The first company we approached was Simply Squeezed. It was one of our main competitors and we believed the brand was enjoying too much freedom with its label claims. We went to meet Steve Brownlie, who owns the brand. We knocked on his door and voiced our concerns with his label and asked him to bring it into line with our perception of the Fair Trading

Act. It was one of our first meetings for Charlie's and ended with us being told to push off and tell someone who cares.

Arano was another. At one stage its labels claimed that the juice was made with the fruit of 20 oranges. It wasn't. It was made with some squeezed juice, yes, but there was also water and added sugar, quite a lot of added sugar, in there. Keri juice, now owned by Coca-Cola, showed fruit stands, like those you might see on rural New Zealand roads, on its TV ad, yet a lot of its concentrate comes from China in drums. It's not, as some might think, made with Kerikeri oranges.

In 2001 we took Steve Brownlie's advice and went to the Commerce Commission and submitted a 20-page document outlining all the issues we had, all the misleading aspects that frustrated us about the New Zealand juice industry. That started a two-year chapter of trying to get something done. The Commission refused to do anything at first. Then it sent out people who knew very little about the juice industry to investigate (I felt for the investigators as they had to try to learn the intricacies of the juice market in a few months; it had taken us years). We had such clear and concise arguments against our competitors, but some of it we believed was not even investigated. It was selective, brushing the surface on a few concerns. Without any knowledge of the juice category, it was very difficult for the Commission to understand the whole market and cope on a complaint-by-complaint basis.

It was hugely time-consuming for us to keep on at the Commission and we used up a hell of a lot of negative energy thinking about what some of our competitors were getting away with in the meantime. We were just three guys — we didn't have a legal team — so time spent on the Commerce Commission issue was time away from building the business.

Stefan Lepionka: There was no one that wanted to support us in it. The likes of the Commerce Commission, the Fair Trading Act, the producers themselves — they all seemed to be happy with the status quo. At the cost of the consumer who is being misled.

We were probably a bit naïve; we believed that the truth would out, and everyone would be pulled into line. Instead we came up against an organisation hampered by red tape, bureaucracy and lily-livered politics. That's consistent with so many things in New Zealand society these days — the rigmarole and red tape that keep people in jobs. I'm sure every industry is the same: I bet it's the same in the legal fraternity, the building trade. That's life. But it was tiresome. Even though I love a good fight, at times it was tempting to just give up. And it was really frustrating to discover the Commerce Commission was just about a waste of time.

The Commerce Commission rules according to whether something is misleading to the average person on the street. That's a great litmus test, but I don't believe they apply it. In 2003 only the small companies — Simply Squeezed and Arano — were prosecuted by the Commerce Commission. They were taken to task for misleading consumers by implying their juices were fresh and made in New Zealand. Simply Squeezed was fined $40,000, which was a joke as that's probably only a week's worth of business for them. We believe the Commission should have ensured Simply Squeezed should have changed the name of its juice, or the contents. As it is, Simply Squeezed is still called Simply Squeezed and is still made with concentrate and water and sugar and preservative and some squeezed juice. We still reckon that's misleading to consumers.

Stefan Lepionka: They were slapped on the hand with a wet bus ticket in a little court in Hawke's Bay, but we saw it as a victory anyway. We think that the act isn't strong enough to deal with these guys. If you finally get to court you will get a guilty plea and the companies get a small fine, but it won't change their business.

Charlie's was investigated by the Commerce Commission too, and we were issued with a warning. The Commission found that our product was 'highly pasteurised' and that consumers didn't necessarily know that. Every product in New Zealand has to be pasteurised. It's the law. That's what kills *E. coli* and other bugs. You do it by heating the product and then cooling it quickly. All juice concentrate undergoes a far more rigorous process that results in the juice evaporating, leaving a glue-like concentrate (about a seventh of the original juice). This process is a damn sight more damaging to the juice than pasteurisation. We squeeze the oranges, put the juice through the pasteurisation process, and then cool it in bottles, sometimes adding vitamin C.

The Commerce Commission has a small budget, and it seemed critically understaffed, so it's my personal belief that it didn't have the manpower to take on the big guys. If it had prosecuted the multinationals, the big guys could have thrown big dollars at their legal teams and told them to drag the issue out in the courts for years. Maybe that's a conspiracy theory, but that was my gut feeling at the time.

The New Zealand Juice and Beverage Association wasn't much help either, but that's no surprise. It's basically run by the big guys: Coca-Cola (which owns Rio juices) and Frucor. I can only say that because I'm out of the business now, but I'm not the only one who thinks that way. Michael Barnett (who also runs the Auckland Chamber of Commerce) stepped down from running the association's compliance committee because, as he said in his resignation letter, 'the make-up of the compliance committee has concerned me, in that it is heavily representative of the large players and fails to reflect the smaller players and new entrants who need a voice'.

To this day we still don't have a properly regulated industry, and Charlie's has to depend on itself to educate shoppers about juice. That's why we campaigned to get a piece on the 'Holmes' show. Pete Cronshaw had a look at the juice industry and what the New Zealand public has to muddle through to understand the various juice brands. We got him over to Australia, where he went through our production facility. It took a lot to get that to happen, but it was worth it if one or two people listened.

It's worth it, too, for us to do comparative advertising. We did a huge amount of research on comparative advertising and we found out that it generally turns New Zealanders off to see people bad-mouthing other brands. We set out not to bad-mouth other juices, but to compare their products with ours. By law you can compare products in a commercial, but you can't insinuate that a competitor's product is inferior. We had to go through a huge process of understanding the legal rights and wrongs of comparative advertising, and make sure that we were bang-on about the claims that we were making. We knew that there was still a risk that people would think we were slagging our competitors off, but that hasn't happened; our television ads have been really effective.

Stefan Lepionka: The advertising was a head-on approach, designed to get people talking about real juice. We took a huge risk with it because New Zealanders don't like organisations knocking other organisations. Immediately the big juice companies were rattled. We had letters coming in thick and fast.

I front all the ads. We shoot a whole lot in an afternoon usually, and I have to do endless re-takes. It's a pretty full-on day because I've got to remember my lines and I've got to deliver them to the satisfaction of the lawyer sitting there, who makes sure the way I hold my eyebrow or grin can't be taken the wrong way or that I could be seen as slighting our competitors.

I think we've done the Charlie's ads in a typically cheeky and irreverent way and perhaps that's why people have liked them. Recently we did a series of ads with a policeman sitting there grilling me about whether or not I'm telling the truth. That's been a successful campaign. I think people see us as ballsy for taking on the brands bigger than us and we're proud to be leading the way in trying to tidy up the industry.

* * *

In September 2003 Paul Holmes had a bit of a blue when he called Kofi Annan a 'cheeky darkie' on his Newstalk ZB radio show. Not surprisingly, Paul's comment ruffled a few feathers in New Zealand. It was a stupid thing to say, a real cock-up, but I think, taken in the context of his career (which has been outstanding for a couple of decades) it wasn't the end of the world. Mitsubishi, sponsor of the 'Holmes' show on television, wasn't impressed though, and pulled out of the programme for fear of seeming politically incorrect.

I'm not a big fan of the politically correct movement; in fact it makes me want to be as non-PC as possible. If there's a contentious issue that

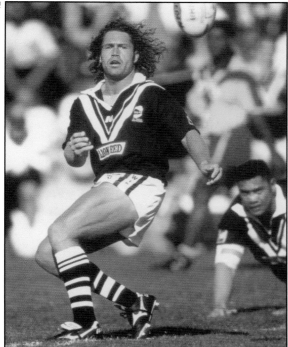

Fortunately the Kiwis-Papua New Guinea test series was held in New Zealand in 1996 . . . over there they were known to throw poisonous snakes into your changing room.

Teaming up again with John Timu in '96.

Good times after the Kiwis' series win against Great Britain in '96.

Getting ready to duck — North Harbour vs Waikato, 1998.

I played against Auckland plenty of times over the years, but tasted victory only a few times. This was one of those occasions, for North Harbour in 1998.

We had a bad Blues season in 1999. By the look on my dial, we are receiving some strong words.

'Get there . . . !'

Playing my last season of first-class rugby back in Dunedin — this time for the Highlanders. I'd had my fun.

Charlie's founders — Simon, Stefan and me enjoying a day out during America's Cup, 2000.

The 'Sports Café' crew, headed by Ric 'Dugong' Salizzo. Beats me how it lasted 10 years.

'Sports Café' a few minutes before going to air. Quite simply, my job was to try to ruin Ric's show.

'Sports Café' — the only show in New Zealand television history where you were paid to drink beer and laugh.

After dark . . . a time where Ridgey is at his most dangerous. This time it's Tokyo.

Group hug with an old Argentine polo legend. For the record, Ridgey lost the polo.

We were told not to stop in the favelas (slums) just outside of Rio de Janeiro, but the film crew and I needed a meal and a few beers. From left: Terry, Steve, Chico (interpreter), me and James.

Ridgey and I with two very capable Argentinean dancers. And again, just for the record, I won the dancing.

Replaying the goal footage from a soccer challenge in Buenos Aires.

Getting ready to learn the tango. Neither Ridgey nor I can really dance.

it would be safer not to discuss, I prefer to discuss it. A bit of healthy debate and unencumbered free thought is just what New Zealand needs, I reckon.

I think the PC environment we live in these days is repressing individuality. It's a form of dumbing down. We treat everyone like morons, because there are just a few morons. We reduce the speed that everyone travels at on the road because there are a few boy racers. We implement liquor bans at the beach over New Year just because there are idiots who light bonfires and drink bourbon straight out of the bottle. Kids can't have lolly scrambles at school any more, because there's a chance that they'll all go for the same lolly and bump heads. Bullrush has been banned in the playground in case a fragile kid gets a hiding. There's no risk allowed in life any more because we anticipate and regulate the behaviour of the lowest common denominator. We live in a really cool country where there's plenty of diversity. Why don't we get on with it and take the handbrake off?

This country is so proud of being unique and we have some of the most liberal thinkers in the world. So why do we have to stifle that individuality? Why do we have to protect against every conceivable injury or hurt? We should let people make decisions for themselves. We've got to stop over-governing everything.

The Aussies have got a cool attitude. They have the advantage over us in that way. While we can be quite reserved and unsure of ourselves, they believe they can do anything and they've got an inherent confidence that isn't corrupted by the PC brigade. In the sporting environment that confidence can turn into arrogance, but at least they want to succeed.

Graham Lowe, the great New Zealand rugby league coach, once told a classic story. He said to a bunch of Australian school kids, 'Who can kick the ball over from the 22?'. They all stuck their hands up and said, 'Me, Me'. He came to New Zealand and asked the same question of a bunch of children, and they all pointed at one kid and said, 'Him'. That to me sums up the difference between us. Aussies all want to have a crack, to try and maybe fail, but to at least give it a shot. Kiwis are more worried about making a dick of themselves, or upsetting someone.

Or maybe they've been handed too many eighth place awards at prize-giving. Whatever the reason, I think we've embraced this whole PC notion with such rigour that we're afraid to take a chance. That's sad, because it removes any individualism, any passion, any risk from everyone's lives. PC to me seems focused on fear. Don't go in the sun or you will get cancer, don't drive too fast, don't drink too much, don't eat the wrong food. In essence, don't do anything that could stop you living a boring, mediocre life to a ripe old age.

The 'Holmes' show was the most powerful piece of TV space in New Zealand and we saw an opportunity to grab it at a good price, regardless of what the PC brigade thought of what Paul said. We knew 'Holmes' would deliver Charlie's message to a huge audience and it would be an opportunity to do something new and exciting. We worried about how we'd make up the dollars, but we thought we had to have a crack. That's always been the Charlie's philosophy. The business had started with nothing, and we were always prepared to risk finishing with nothing too.

Stefan Lepionka: As a company we had no budget for marketing, yet we had to get our story out there to consumers. We realised this was the ideal way to do it. We couldn't afford it, but we decided to get the sponsorship deal first, and then find out how to afford it.

We went to TVNZ and said, 'We back Paul Holmes, we think he's a great guy despite his cock-up, and he deserves a second chance'. We had a sound business plan and we sold the idea to TVNZ. We got the sponsorship at a subsidised rate. Then we had to make it work.

With the help of Graeme Hunter, a media strategist, we devised a plan to get Jeep onboard to share the cost. Jeep had lent me a vehicle six months earlier and I thought it could be a really good opportunity for them and Charlie's. It would be the first car company on 'Holmes' since Mitsubishi.

Jeep liked the idea of showing the off-road capabilities of their vehicles and jumped in. It advertised within our ads — as a prize under the guise of a Charlie's promotion. That gave us back some of the revenue the sponsorship cost. We had a whale of a time making the ad. By the end of the day we had basically trashed a brand-new truck.

We did something quite different with our sponsorship — we told a different story every single night at the top of the 'Holmes' show: 'Tonight "Holmes" is brought to you by the letter "E". "E" for excitement. We'd like to share our excitement at being the new sponsor of "Holmes"; "Holmes" is brought to you by the letter "C". "C" is for China, where our fruit juice doesn't come from. Not from concentrate, and certainly not from China.'

Stefan Lepionka: It was so risky at the time. It was also controversial, but it got our message across. And it's been one of the reasons our brand has been so successful.

We were the first FMCG (fast-moving consumer good) to sponsor the show. And really quickly our brand awareness went from below 50 per cent to 95 per cent. We were right up there with a product like Red Bull. It was a superb deal for us. And it proved our 'have a crack' philosophy worked.

* * *

There are so many things I learnt in sport that have stood me in good stead for business. After all, business is probably the most competitive environment there is after sport. I learnt in sport to be competitive, to strive for goals, to be single-minded and not ruthless at the expense of others, but ruthless in the pursuit of goals.

In New Zealand, perhaps more than other countries, integrity is the key in business. It's such a small country: shit on someone just once and that can come back to bite you in the bum. I think you've got to be ethical, honest and upfront. Better to run the risk of being naïve, rather than being after the buck no matter the cost. And you've got to be very lucky, or very skilled, for it all to last.

If you're competitive in the business environment the yardstick tends to be the money you make. That's the measure of whether you're more successful than the other person. Stefan derives a huge amount of self-worth out of business. That's his yardstick. He gets his kicks from work. He puts a lot into it, and he gets a lot out of it. He'll never sit on his hands and he'll never admit defeat. He's a really aggressive CEO. He knows what he wants and what time he wants to do it in, and it's always attack, attack, attack. He's the most gifted businessman I've come across.

Simon is Mr Honest, the first to work and the last to leave. He constantly plays down his own successes in the company because he's keen to divert attention, but without him we would have been absolutely poked on many occasions.

Stefan Lepionka: Marc thinks anything's possible. He's a jetfighter. He doesn't see the benefit in going slowly and using excessive strategy. That philosophy is always the same, whether in business or in his personal life. Once we were out fishing in the Coromandel. Marc was driving the boat. It was cold and as we were coming back into Opito Bay, and it was getting rough as guts, Marc decided to drive the boat straight in and up onto the sand without stopping, like he'd seen in the movies. If he'd thought about it logically, he would have known it wasn't going to work, but he came hooning into the bay. I was holding onto the rail for dear life and when we hit the sand I thought I'd lost my fingers. Simon nearly went through the front window. That's Marc's can-do, take-on-the-world attitude. And there are so many of those sorts of stories about him.

Building the business has been a bloody hard row to hoe and every time we've had a setback we've thought, 'What a bastard, we really needed that to happen'. But I've learnt that the harder it is, the more you feel like you deserve it when you finally break through. That was how we felt when we got Charlie's into service stations. Our competitors tried to prevent us from getting exposure there. They'd do deals that would block our products. In 2004, Shell gave us a break because they believed we had earned the opportunity. When we finally got in there and Charlie's started outselling all the other juices, we knew we deserved it. We'd worked bloody hard to get Shell to support us; we didn't have a big chequebook to buy the space — it was a huge thrill.

We've made some mistakes. We launched a three-litre juice range on gut feel. We thought that because our one-litre was selling at $2.99, a three litre could sell at $4.99. It didn't work, because Coca-Cola lowered the price of its Rio juice and we couldn't compete. Our three-litre rocked off the shelves when we put it at a promotional price, but we couldn't afford to keep it that low and we ended up deleting it.

It was the same with Charlie's sports water. We came up with the idea of water sweetened with apple juice, instead of added sugar. Just as we were about to launch it, Coca-Cola launched Aquana, a similar product, into a handful of supermarkets. Our point of difference — no sugar added — was lost overnight. I don't know if Coca-Cola caught wind of what we were doing, or if it was coincidence; either way it was incredibly bad timing and our water needed to be addressed pronto. It was an example of us being too aggressive and not getting it right (and we're working on a new water product now).

By 2005 Simon, Stefan and I started thinking about taking Charlie's public. The idea behind listing on the Stock Exchange was that it would give us exposure to more finance and help us grow exponentially.

Stefan Lepionka: Marc and I, in simple terms, kept running out of money. We'd sunk so much money into Charlie's, and we had big aspirations, so we had to raise money somehow. We thought listing was probably the best vehicle because it would give people a chance to get behind the brand. So we went down the traditional listing route.

You can't just charge into the NZX50. You have to make the grade. The advice we were getting from people in the know was that we were too small for the NZX50, but that we might be able to get on the smaller, secondary exchange. That was a blow. So we went down the private equity track for a little while, only to realise we wanted freedom, and to have investors for the long term rather than the short term, so that wasn't going to work.

Fortunately, Spectrum Resources came along. It was a company that was already listed, that had some money in the bank but was floundering. We did a reverse takeover: effectively Spectrum bought Charlie's, then changed its name to Charlie's, leaving us trading in its place. At the end of the deal Charlie's owned 85 per cent of Spectrum, got a cash injection, and got listed on the NZX50.

The logistics of listing a company on the Stock Exchange make for a time-consuming process, especially with the due diligence that was required to ascertain the value of our company and the value of Spectrum. It was worth it. It meant we punched above our weight yet again and still had control of our own destiny. We also set up our own sales force so that we weren't dependent on a third party for distribution.

Stefan Lepionka: It's meant we have more governance. Part of listing means that you have to share information, you have to have processes in place and advisors. We ran a board table from day one; we would have board meetings with zero turnover. It was part of building governance for the business. But with listing on the Stock Exchange the whole company had to grow up almost overnight.

Stefan, Simon and I had always had it in mind that we'd like to start acquiring companies once we could afford it. The idea was to get the smaller guys, roll them up into Charlie's, and create a really big third player to take on the likes of Frucor and Coke. Together, we thought, we could all be a real force to reckon with.

We'd already done a deal with Red Bull to do its distribution in supermarkets. That was a key win. It meant that our reps were going into stores armed with another quality beverage in the same category. And after going public, Charlie's acquired Phoenix Organics. Phoenix is a great little company. It has done a great job and done it ethically. It has a key point of difference — organic products — but one that works well with Charlie's products, and buying Phoenix doubled Charlie's size.

It was rapid growth. In a year we went from the three of us and an assistant, to 70-odd staff. We had our own sales and marketing team, and a finance department. Staff had to have employment contracts and be managed. That's not my thing — I don't like to spend most of my time worrying about what other people are doing. Simon and Stefan are better at that. I prefer being my own boss.

Charlie's now had more than 30 products and I started to realise that the logistics of managing those and marketing and sales wasn't me. I was doing a job Charlie's could employ someone else to do and I probably wasn't doing it as well as someone else could. I was pretty good at the big picture — where we wanted the brand to go — but the actual fundamental steps, the details, weren't my strong point. I was effective in creating opportunities, cultivating personal contacts, but the semantics of the marketing job weren't something I was overly skilled at, nor did I enjoy them. I believed we should hire someone to take on that responsibility. Besides, I didn't enjoy being tied to a desk, sitting behind a computer 50 hours a week. I wanted to be doing something different every day, to have a range of opportunities on the go. I don't like to be locked into a box, a job description. Business isn't everything to me. It's a passion, but it's not the be all and end all.

Stefan Lepionka: Marc's lazy about the stuff that bores him. Everyone has strengths and weaknesses. With the governance comes an expectation that you'll do the boring stuff too and he didn't enjoy it. Towards the end the business was doing his head in a bit.

I made the decision to quit in 2005, about two weeks before I went to England and Russia to film 'Rocky Road'. In reality I should have made that decision earlier but I wanted to stick it out. I was about to be away from the office for two months. That was adding to the pressure we were under. I realised I couldn't do justice to a fulltime role at Charlie's and spend months offshore filming; it was time to step back. I would remain one of the biggest shareholders, stay on the board of directors, and front the Charlie's ads, but I would resign from the day-to-day involvement in Charlie's.

A few months later I was convicted on possession of a Class B drug, and had to step down from the board. At the AGM later that year, there was an opportunity to get back onto the board. They'd done the research and discovered that 97 per cent of Charlie's consumers still consumed the brand despite my conviction. That was pretty encouraging.

Returning to the board would give me a role in the future of the business. It was a company that I started, so of course I cared about it, but I also knew that things had changed at Charlie's. It was a public company so it had to have a more measured approach; there were investors to keep happy. I knew I could achieve just as much over a coffee or a beer with the directors as I would at AGMs. I didn't need the constraint of having to be in New Zealand every month to attend a board meeting. I didn't want to be in a position where I wasn't a proactive member of the board. I decided to make a clean break.

Stefan Lepionka: I don't know that it was a good decision for him not to come back on. I would have preferred him to. People voted him back in, but he decided not to come back. He has other interests. Marc and I are still the two biggest shareholders of Charlie's to this day. But he has the freedom to do what he wants to do, and remain the spokesman.

I miss hanging out with my mates, but leaving was the right decision for me. I like my life to be in chapters. When I was playing rugby I saw it as a cool chapter in my life that, once it was over, I would move on from. Charlie's has come from nothing, from an idea inside our heads, to being a multi-million-dollar juice company in six short years. We've worked bloody hard to do it and we've had a lot of fun along the way. But it was time to move on. I still keep myself informed about Charlie's, and I'll always have a huge interest in it but, in a way, that chapter's over.

On the Telly

My first television experience was disappointing. In 1993, while I was playing for Otago and living in Dunedin, I got a call from Touchdown Productions asking if I'd be interested in doing a spot on 'Mountain Dew on the Edge'. The idea was that I'd spend a night in a snow cave and I presumed that meant I'd spend the night with the presenter, Lana Coc-Kroft. Naturally, I was pretty excited at the thought of that, so I jumped at the chance and ran around telling all my mates I was off to share a snow cave with an ex-Miss New Zealand.

I got down to the Pisa Range, out the back of Queenstown, and it was freezing, absolutely freezing. After half an hour or so of meeting all the crew and whizzing around on Skidoos, I politely enquired about Lana. 'She's not coming,' someone said. I'd be digging my own hole and sleeping in it alone, freezing my balls off in the middle of a mountain range. I felt totally ripped off. So it was just as well I didn't have to sleep in the cave at all: I dug it and climbed into it on-camera, then when filming stopped I hopped out and was taken to a lodge for the night. The next day I was filmed coming out of it as if I'd actually spent the night there. That, I learnt, is the magic of television.

Three years later, just after I joined the Warriors, Matthew Ridge asked me if I'd team up with him for 'Ansett New Zealand Time of Your Life'. Julie Christie had asked him to be a presenter on the show and suggested he find someone to do it with, so he asked me.

Julie Christie, director, owner of Touchdown Productions: I was looking for an offsider for him for a new television show. The idea was that Zinzan Brooke would be Matthew's foil, but we couldn't get him to do it, so Matthew suggested Marc.

Ridgey and I didn't know each other very well, but we had hit it off at training. He was an ex-All Black like me, and had helped make sure my transition to league was OK. I had leaned on him and his experience to understand where I was going.

People love to hate Ridgey in a funny sort of way. The public perception of him is that he's brash and a bit arrogant. He's not like that at all; he just has no time for bullshit, and couldn't care less what people think of him. I've always been quite the opposite, worrying a bit that people see me as a nice guy, but I like that honesty about Ridgey, that 'what you see is what you get' type of attitude. He's a decent dude. And a survivor. We're great mates and we have each other's best interests at heart.

Julie Christie: They're very different characters. Marc's more of a contained character. He might not seem that way, but he doesn't expose himself as much as Matthew. Their chemistry was instant, because they both have a similar sense of humour. It's very difficult for me to think of them separately now.

For our first ever segment on 'Time of Your Life', we kayaked from Auckland to Rangitoto Island. From then on we had a little segment each week where we'd go and do something fun, like a bungy jump in Queenstown or aerobatics in an old plane. I'm not a great one for heights, but you can't help but have fun going out and filming something like that, it's just such an adrenalin rush. And being filmed didn't bother us, probably because we were used to cameras and the media from our rugby days. We were able to think that the guy holding the camera was just a guy holding a camera, and we didn't really think too in-depth about it going into people's living rooms.

I didn't really know how TV worked, and in the beginning I could never understand why it took so long to film stuff. In television there's a lot of waiting around with your thumb up your arse, waiting for the right light, the traffic to go past, or the sound guy to be ready. Ridgey can't sit still, he's like a kid with ADD, so I loved winding him up about all the mucking around. 'Jeez these buggers are taking a while,' I'd say to him and eventually he'd get so wound up that he'd explode and start growling at the camera crew. We'd come from the sporting environment, where you just take the piss out of everyone relentlessly, and so we did that with the crew too, and pretty soon there were a few people who didn't want to work with us.

Julie Christie: They had a very difficult reputation in the early days. They're a fairly intimidating pair of characters. People were afraid of them. They were just too impatient and they didn't understand the process, nor want to. They like to dominate whomever they work with. They want to get their own way. They've always set their own rules.

In those days we were given scripts that we were supposed to follow. It would take about 12 takes to get it right and Ridgey and I invariably reckoned the ones that veered off-script had more personality, but the directors always disagreed — they wanted it verbatim. We would get so frustrated having to do it over and over again to get it right. After about a year Julie relented and since then we've ad-libbed our lines. It's a hell of a lot more enjoyable that way.

Julie Christie: They don't have a lot of the discipline required for television. They hate doing the second take. They are useless at preparation. You might as well not bother sending them the script, as they'll never follow it.

The early ratings showed a peak in viewers during our segment of 'Time of Your Life'. That led to us getting our own show, 'Fresh Up In the Deep End'.

Julie Christie: They were an unbelievable instant hit. Their blokey, 'mine's bigger than yours' sense of humour struck a chord straight away with New Zealanders. They struck a chord with ordinary people.

We were stoked to get that because it gave us the opportunity to do a bit more of what we loved doing, going around New Zealand trying all kinds of things. The premise of the show was that we were to be sent out on missions. We got to take Rachel Hunter to a photo shoot in my old Chevy. We hung out with Jordan Luck and the Exponents and recorded a song. And we did stints as circus clowns and private detectives.

We'd yarn to people, but our primary aim was always to make fun of ourselves. You've got to be able to have a crack at yourself, not take yourself too seriously — and invariably the joke's on us. I think there are a few shows on TV at the moment where the joke's always on somebody else and I think that Kiwis don't buy into that too much.

Julie Christie: I came up with a scheme that the camera would always be the third mate with them. That is a really important part of their success. It's never an in-joke or inward thing with them. It's about the audience laughing with them, never them laughing at them. They're very good at that.

One of the funniest days on 'In the Deep End' was at the Highland Games in Dunedin. I was quite excited to go back to Dunedin, my old stomping ground, and have a night down at the Gardies. Ridgey was excited because I'd been raving about the place. We got down there and sat around a big banquet table in a big old Gothic hall, with these guys dressed up as Scottish warriors, who were about to launch into the Highland Games. The idea was that we would toast them with a wee dram. We probably attacked it with a bit more vigour than we should have. We kept intentionally screwing up the lines just after we'd drunk the shot glass, so we'd have to do another take. After six or seven takes, we were a little worse for wear. Or at least Ridgey was. I'd honed my drinking skills to a fine art at varsity, so sitting down for a whisky or two wasn't a problem for me, but Ridgey's a hopeless drinker.

I ended up having to deliver his lines as well as my own. Julie, who'd very wisely come down to keep an eye on us, wasn't impressed.

The same thing happened when we went to the Kumara races, although I was the one who was shickered that time. We arrived in Kumara, did a bit of filming, then the crew told us to take off for a few hours and have a bit of fun before we had to film the last scene. We did exactly that. My experience has always been that the further south you go the better the people you meet and we certainly enjoyed the great hospitality of the local West Coasters that afternoon. When we reconvened to film a farewell scene my ability to deliver my lines was slightly impaired and Matthew had to do the whole lot. It was a bit of a bloody dag.

* * *

Not long after the show started, I became aware that people were recognising me in public. A few people — people who followed rugby — knew who I was when I played for Otago and the All Blacks, but not many, and now I would walk down the street or be in the middle of my shopping at the supermarket, and feel people looking at me. It was a really weird feeling and something I hadn't even considered when I decided to do TV. To be honest, I hadn't known what the hell I was getting myself into.

Julie Christie: Marc managed to become a personality when he was still playing sport. That was unheard of in those days — it was a very restrictive time in New Zealand sport. Rugby completely suppressed personalities. All Blacks were part of a team and didn't stand out. He broke down that barrier. He developed a life after football. Now he's the guy that mothers want their daughters to bring home and their fathers do too.

Chris Ellis: He's extremely unpretentious and I think that's what people like about him. He certainly doesn't pose, never has done.

Not long after that Mandy told me that she wanted to do some television. I told her to think about it really carefully, because I'd learnt that you can't put a price on your anonymity. Once it happens, once you're in everyone's living room each week, you can't do anything about it, even if it's not something you've desired.

I didn't find it easy in the beginning, but I knew there was no sense in worrying about it. It was a matter of put up or shut up, because it came with the job. And there were tremendous upsides to it. I met some cool people and was offered some great opportunities because of my public profile. Years later, when we started Charlie's, launching our brand was a lot easier because I was a recognisable personality. The downside is it can be quite invasive.

It's not a big deal, but some days I have a shit day and when somebody comes up to say gidday I don't feel like a chat. When that happens I've got two options; to say 'Piss off'; or to smile and have a bit of a chat. My parents taught me to see myself as others see me. That's been bloody good advice and it's why I've always done the latter in that situation — said gidday and stopped for a yarn. That's come naturally 99 per cent of the time, because I think if people are going out of their way then the least you can do is return the favour, even if you don't feel like it. I think that's an attitude that has helped me out.

Since 'In the Deep End' Ridgey and I have been lucky enough to always have a show on the go. One we got involved in was a show called 'The Mating Game'. Ridgey and I were each given a guy or a girl to send off on a blind date. They'd have an earpiece and every now and again we'd give them a bit of advice. It was supposed to be highly competitive between the two of us, as to who did the best on their blind date. There was nothing that wasn't rehearsed in that show, so it was completely contrived. There was no freedom for us to have a bit of fun; there was no personality. It was just ridiculous. I mean, who would take any advice from Matthew or me about dating? It was really, really bad and before it even went to air we knew it was going to be a real lemon, but it was too late to get out of it.

We've been doing 'Game of Two Halves' for a decade now and that's where Ridgey really hates losing. He's incredibly competitive. I don't know another person as competitive as me, aside from him, and we will both fight to the bitter end on anything.

Julie Christie: They're the perfect foil for each other. They are better together than they are individually. And they just love beating each other. Marc is faster and stronger; Matthew is more agile. So it's a constant challenge. That keeps them going.

In the early days of 'Game' it would be fiercely intense. During the breaks, while the cameras were off, everyone would be blowing up, kicking stuff, screaming and swearing. I wish people could see the behind-the-scenes footage of those breaks.

We've got the filming of each episode down to a fine art now and it is still a thrill to beat Ridgey on that show. He definitely hasn't won more games than me. I know because in the early series I got on well with one of the researchers. He'd put the answers up on a screen only visible from my side. It would run the answers, so when Eric Young asked a question we'd sneak a look. To make it look realistic we'd lose the odd game on purpose, but Mike King and I cheated constantly for about two years and Ridgey didn't know. When he did find out — holy shit, I've never seen a tantrum like it.

Matthew Ridge: I've won more than Marc — I've won for the last three years. And when I found out he was cheating, all hell broke loose. It doesn't matter who you are, you're going to get a hard time on that show because we're so competitive. That's why it's hard to get guests on. They can't get a word in. And they don't want to be abused.

Humiliating or causing pain to Ridgey is one of my greatest joys. Our 'Rocky Road' series makes the most of that rivalry between us. We've done some brilliant things on that show: we've been to Ninja school in Japan, and sumo-wrestled, we went to circus school in South America, played polo, and took dancing lessons. Most recently we went to Russia, which was pretty average. Russia's a tough place to visit and a hard place to work. It was very difficult for us to film anything that looked any good at all, which was a bit bloody frustrating, and the Russians were keen to take our money at any opportunity. You can tell that life is cheap in that country; get yourself in the wrong place at the wrong time and you're in real trouble. We were there for 10 days when a friend from Zurich called and gave me the phone number of a mate of his who was working in Moscow and our last three days there were absolutely fantastic because our guide ensured we didn't leave a stone unturned.

Making a TV series is a job, and it's sometimes hard work. You work long days and, when you're away on location, don't get many days off. We have a huge amount of fun too. We're lucky because we've pulled together a crew of really good guys and that makes a big difference.

Julie Christie: They've been very good with ideas. The schemes they come up with are magic. When you go on the road you can always presume they'll come up with something.

We get an allowance for accommodation, which is enough for a three-star hotel usually, but Ridgey and I always pool our money and get a nice five-star room together, just like you would if you were on a footie trip. It suits me because I like to have someone around to bounce off and we have a bloody good time, telling a few stories, having some laughs. It ensures constant hilarity, from the moment we finish filming for the day. We'll go for a meal, out on the ran-tan, then come back and spin yarns until we fall asleep.

In the early series of 'Rocky Road' I'd be livid if I lost a challenge, particularly if it was something that I thought I should have won. Ridgey was probably an even worse loser than me and there were times we'd have to stop filming and wait for him to calm down after a loss.

Ridgey still moans and groans constantly about the cheese rolling. He claims I duped him by saying I was going to take it easy, and then running my heart out and winning the thing. Really he should have known me better than taking me at my word; is there ever anything that we've competed in that I haven't given 100 per cent? No.

Matthew Ridge: We drove for flipping hours to find this cheese-rolling place and then we walked for about an hour to get to the base of the summit of the hill. We climbed it, with the crew, and about half an hour before the start of the race, as we were ready to put on numbers, Marc says, 'No, I can't do it'.

The day before, we'd been doing the high jump with the female decathlon champion of England and I'd hurt my knee. More people get injured doing the cheese rolling than the Running of the Bulls in Spain. It's a 200-metre slope and it's basically at a 45-degree angle. It takes 10 seconds to get to the bottom, so basically you are going twice the speed of someone like Carl Lewis. We watched the first race and people were falling down and getting munted, breaking bones and being taken away in ambulances. So I said, 'I can't do it mate, my knee's poked', and I went back down to the bottom.

Matthew Ridge: I was furious because I didn't want to give up, and I thought it was one of the first things we'd done that I had a fair chance of winning. So when Marc came back up and said he'd do it after all, I said, 'Right mate, we'll just take it easy because we don't want to hurt ourselves. Let's just make sure we get down the bottom in one piece.' Then he just took off! He flew out of the blocks. There was no way I was going to catch him. I was swearing and cursing behind him, running as fast as I could and falling on my arse. He got in the lead and then took a massive roll. He went up in the air and came tumbling down and smacked his head on the ground, but he got up and continued to run. He came first and I came third. He got onto TV all over the world and every newspaper in London.

Ric Salizzo: The thing about Marc is that he has incredible balance. He can do things that no one else can do. That's on the field and in his drunken antics too. He would have made a great midget acrobat.

The fuss after the event was quite overwhelming. I was the champ, the cheese-rolling champ, and Ridgey was hating it. I've never had so much attention. Straight after, there were about eight news cameras thrust in my face and all of these journalists lining up to interview me. That just made Ridgey even more beside himself. He came charging over while I was being interviewed and said, 'I got third', I said, 'Mate, look, you got fifth, push off', which really wound him through the roof. I loved it. I had mates calling me up from all around the world saying, 'Jesus, you just won the cheese rolling'. It was probably the biggest fuss of my sporting career, winning a race down a hill chasing a cheese!

But the most important win that day was over Matthew because he was so upset.

In Amsterdam we met up with a professional baseball team. Being a bit of a cricketer I thought I'd beat Ridgey quite comfortably. He went in to bat first. The pitcher came out and he threw a few dollies down and Ridgey managed to get onto a couple of them. Ridgey started to brag about how good he was, which embarrassed the pitcher, so when I came out to bat he started opening up on his arm and throwing down fastballs. He started pitching at the edge of the plate, so I had to reach for them. I kept missing them and I started to get really shitty — not as shitty as I would have got a few years earlier, but it still really hurt.

The viewers tend to take sides on 'Rocky Road'. They either want me to win, or they want Ridgey to win, and if one of us loses they want to see the other one punished for it. A whack over the hamstrings, a blowdart in the arse, a few lashes — that's what they like to see. Causing your mate any degree of pain is hugely motivating, I think. And Ridgey's a good sport. That's one thing I'll give him; he does take his punishment like a man.

In Russia, for one of my punishments, Ridgey woke me up with a shot from a Taser gun. He snuck into the room while I was asleep and zapped me. That was not pleasant at all. My whole body cramped up and I was kind of paralysed. There was a lot of screaming — me with pain and Ridgey with delight.

I got him back: while we were in Russia we had a competition to see who could stay in the sauna longest. The sauna was hot, not like a sauna in New Zealand. So much steam comes out it feels like you're cooking. I won and Ridgey's punishment was to get five pinkies on the back. When you're really hot, having come out of a bath or a sauna like that, a pinkie really hurts. I held nothing back and aimed five slaps on the same spot.

Probably the worst punishment I had to endure was a Brazilian wax. There was a knock at my hotel room door at about 6 a.m. and in comes Ridgey with this huge, bearded woman. He'd organised this behemoth of a Brazilian to come in and wax my front porch as my punishment. 'Mate, you've taken it too far, there's certain things that people want to see and certain things that people don't want to see and this is one of them,' I told him. But I had to go through with it. This woman didn't even use hot wax (which I'm told is better); she used cold wax strips. I think she got some sick sort of enjoyment out of it. Oh, it was awful. I had to clamp my bits down between my legs while she worked. The pain was excruciating. I now have a healthy respect for what women go through; if I was a woman I'd go straight back to the 1970s afro, the au naturel look. I got my own back by making Ridgey a stick-on pube moustache from the hairs on the wax strips. I made him wear it down Copacabana Beach, propositioning women while in his Speedos.

Ridgey loves any opportunity to show off his body. When we went to Athens for 'Rocky Road', we'd rip off to the beach when filming was over for the day. I'd be there in my boardies, like any normal New Zealand man, and he'd strip off to a pair of Speedos. It was so wrong. I'd have to move my lounger away from him. And when he hitched his budgie-smugglers up his arse like a G-string so he could get some colour in the cheeks, I packed my stuff up and went back to the hotel.

In England we went wing walking, which involves being strapped to the wing of a plane and doing acrobatics in mid-air. I hate heights, but I can't show any fear on the show. I was pretty bloody nervous this particular time. These two girls, who called themselves the Ugly Ducklings, turned up and off we went. We knew that the loser was going to have to go up again and wing walk in a woman's pink G-string. Ridgey basically lost on purpose, so he could get his kit off and jump into a G-string in front of the ladies.

During the same series Ridgey drove a tank over a parked car. In a tank, you've got a thing about the size of your finger — a joystick — that dictates the direction. We were doing a slalom course in the tank, and we had to go through the course without knocking over the drums on the side. That's quite a hard thing to do because you're looking through a gap the size of a letterbox slot and you've got that tiny joystick that dictates the movement and the speed and the direction. You need to have quite a bit of guidance and instruction before you go in there and give it a whirl. I'd been in first and been given the spiel by the instructor. Ridgey, being a bit more impatient, said, 'Yeah, yeah, I've got it', and jumped in. The moron kicked the thing into reverse and drove over a car.

I don't watch any of our shows unless I stumble across them, but every now and then, when I see one, it's quite interesting to see how it's been edited and put together. TV's something I've had a load of fun doing, but it's not the be all and end all for me. Over the years I've picked up that there's a hell of a lot of political to-ing and fro-ing in the television industry. Ridgey and I have been bloody lucky; we've been able to do it while just being ourselves. That allows us to take the mick, have fun, and not worry about the politics. We just hope people enjoy watching what we get up to.

'Sweating Like a Rapist'

I have been the bane of Ric Salizzo's life for the past 10 years on 'Sports Café'. My job, as far as I could tell, was to cause Ric as much trouble as I could from day dot, and I think I've succeeded pretty well. I've made him blow up several times. I just wish I had a dollar for every time I've got under his skin.

In 1996, Ric phoned me and explained he was starting a sports show. I knew him pretty well from his days as the All Blacks' media liaison person, and he was a guy I always enjoyed hanging out with on tour because he was just such a good bugger. He wanted Zinzan Brooke and John Kirwan as the regulars on his new show, but JK was away for the filming of the pilot, so my name got thrown up and I was asked to fill in.

'It's just a chat show,' Ric said. Me, Ric, Zinny and a woman called Tania (who was supposed to keep us under control, I think) were to be the presenters. We filmed the first episode out at Sky Television in Mt Wellington in Auckland. I got there and in the make-up room stumbled across a heinous old 1970s suit with the wide collar lapels, so I put that on. I thought it would be good to be dressed in something so revolting, pretending to be serious, as if I were on a real sports show.

That first show was one of the most appalling things in television history. I can't believe it even went to air. Ric looked incredibly nervous. There were a couple of really foul pregnant pauses. At one stage Ric said, 'Ah, ah, over to you Tania', and threw her a complete hospital pass. She had to choke her way through until we went to the break. It was beautifully awkward.

Ric Salizzo: The pilot was really crap, but as soon as we put Marc on it was a different kind of show. You could see Marc had a spark, that he worked really well. When we started it was going to be a relaxed but semi-serious sports show, but Marc in his old suit set the tone for the next 10 years and took the show in a whole new direction. When the filming of the next show came around I knew I was going to have to tell JK that Marc was doing it.

From there 'Sports Café' evolved. Ric was the guy in charge and I was the guy who was trying to ruin Ric's show, to sabotage it and bring it down. It was still really low-grade television, but it was funny because we found it amusing, and the worse it was, the funnier it was. It became more polished over the years and found its niche, but it was still the antithesis of other TV shows. On every other show on TV the presenters are polished and smooth and say all the right things. I think that's probably partly why people enjoyed 'Sports Café'. That was the beauty of it; if you were screwing up people enjoyed it more than if you were getting it right.

Graeme Hill joined us early on and started producing the sports clips and that was one of my favourite parts of the show. He's the only guy in New Zealand who can do that — put together those clips with the commentary running over the top of them — and actually take the piss in such a beautiful way. It's very clever. Before long he came on the set as a regular. I liked Graeme's line of questioning because it would invariably lead to a smart-arse climax. Sometimes it would work and other times it wouldn't and it was equally funny whatever the outcome. Even if the question had been a horrible failure he would keep on going with it, which I found funny. Sometimes he'd get shut down by Ric or Lana, but I'd know exactly where he was going to be going with that question if he'd been allowed to get away with it. He and I had a lot of laughs.

Ric Salizzo: It was a bit like a sitcom: Marc was our Kramer — he only had to walk onto the set and people started laughing. He was constantly taking the show off on tangents. I'd fight that for a while on each episode, then he'd bring me over to the dark side; I could never help wanting to go where Marc wanted to go. That's where Lana came in: she would pull me back from going to the dark side.

After the snow-cave kerfuffle I was still keen to meet Lana, so when she was suggested for the show I said, 'Shit hot'. She fitted in right from the outset. It was a nice dynamic.

The time she fell in the mud in our team-building exercise was a cracker. The Human Cannonball decided to take the 'Sports Café' 'team' on a team-building exercise, which involved a bit of off-roading. Afterwards, in a 'trust exercise', we all had to link hands over a big muddy hole and Lana was supposed to fall back into our arms, trusting we would catch her. She fell back and the Cannonball lost his footing and started slipping. He dropped Lana into the puddle and then fell on top of her, which was quite beautiful really. She was covered from head to toe in stagnant mud, and so was the Cannonball. That was splendid.

The good thing about Lana is she's a bit of a tomboy; she doesn't mind getting her hands dirty. She has a good sense of humour and she took all of that stuff on the chin. Well, maybe not all of it. She used to get a bit pissed off. It went down pretty badly when I asked her what her name was spelt backwards. The stupid thing about that was that she fed me that line, by saying, 'Whatever you do, don't ask me what my name is spelt backwards'. I said, 'Oh, thank you so much', and promptly asked her on air. How could I not have used that against her?

Another laugh was when we had the surfers on. I was trying to paint a scene of surfing, of a huge wave about to smash Maz Quinn, so I asked him, 'When you are lying on your stomach and you look behind and you are about to get pounded, what goes through your mind?'. Maz started answering and I said, 'Actually mate, I was asking Lana'.

The first time I saw Eva the Bulgarian was at a pub called York Street in Parnell. She walked in and all the boys in the bar noted her arrival, and then proceeded to fall over each other to talk to her. The following week, Ric told me he'd stumbled across this Bulgarian girl who would make a great interviewer on the show. It was the same girl.

In the beginning Eva could hardly speak a word of English, so her interviews were barely understandable, but she became very popular with 'Sports Café' fans.

We always had a live audience. In the early days at Sky we'd turn up and there'd be 50 people in the audience. They must have been family or friends or something, because quite frankly how they sat through an hour of that in the beginning I don't know.

I like live TV. It gets my adrenalin pumping a wee bit. I know that if I make a cock-up I'm going to have to be pretty quick on my feet to get out of it. And that if I can push somebody else into making a cock-up, they're going to have to be pretty quick too. That suits my style. And my role.

I'd ask absurd questions or wind Lana up, basically do anything to disrupt the show. Ric was quite anal about how long we could speak to each guest. Carol, our floor manager, controlled that by telling us when we had one minute to go. When she'd signal one minute to go I'd invariably start asking a barrage of questions so it pushed the segment way over time and completely ruined the programme plan. That would wind Ric into an absolute frenzy, which would give me real pleasure.

Occasionally, I would come up with an idea and say to Ric, 'OK, when I ask this I want you to say that', but because none of us could act, the pre-rehearsed jokes would always fall flat. There would just be absolute silence, which was a beautifully awful feeling.

I'd always be late for the show (that poor timekeeping again). That was a constant pain in the neck for Ric because everyone else got there an hour and a half before and had a rehearsal. I'd run in 15 minutes before, if I was lucky. There were times I'd get there 10 minutes late — Ric really didn't appreciate that.

Naturally, the guests could make or break the show. You could tell within five minutes whether or not they were going to be good guests, and whether you could take the piss or had to play it straight up and down because they were a bit sensitive. Some guests were fantastic; they wanted to have a yarn and were quite loose about it.

It was difficult sometimes to come up with new angles, particularly if the guest had already been on the show three or four times. I found it hard interviewing rugby players. I couldn't take the mick out of them because they were usually a lot bigger than me, and because New Zealand is so passionate about rugby; if I tried, I'd generally get a lukewarm response.

George Best was brilliant. He came on three-quarters steamed, said what he wanted and pushed off, which was exactly what you would have expected George Best to do.

Nick Faldo was as boring as bat shit. He couldn't understand or interpret the show. He thought that it should be a professional sports show and expected to be asked specific golf questions. Golf's a great game, but talking about it bores me to tears.

Invariably, the Australian sportspeople were great. I don't know what it is, but they seem to speak with a confidence that some of the New Zealand sportspeople don't have. New Zealanders can go into their shell a wee bit, be a little bit more humble. I guess that's more the Kiwi way. But the Aussies have a confidence in front of the camera which allows you to ask them almost anything. Some of them were pretty amusing too, so they enjoyed giving a cheeky reply. Probably my favourite guest ever was The Walrus, big Merv Hughes.

Ric Salizzo: Marc got bored with the sports stuff because he not only knew the questions but also the answers. He knew what it was like to be a rugby player. The rest of us probably felt that way too, but we pretended a bit better.

I far preferred guests who weren't necessarily sports-related. Elle Macpherson was an obvious highlight. She was the hottest chick in the world at the time I interviewed her. I gave her a can of Speight's (she gave me a smile and knocked the top off it) and a crayfish that we'd caught and boiled up specially.

Wing was probably one of my favourite guests. She was an Asian singer from Auckland who I spotted on the Internet. I knew immediately we simply had to get her on the show, so I phoned Wing up and recruited her services. She sang a couple of her favourite tunes. That's a unique musical experience. Let's be honest, she sounds like a strangled cat. And that's the beauty of what she does. It was hard to know how to take it, but by the end she was getting a standing ovation, people were getting right in behind it. She loved it. We asked her back for the final show and she gave us a beautiful rendition of AC/DC's 'Highway to Hell'.

Ric Salizzo: With each script I would try to make sure there was stuff that amused Marc because it was no good me doing a show focused on what I found interesting. He'd get bored and say so and our viewers would agree and switch off. I had to try to keep him entertained, like giving a toy to a kid. There were a lot of things that Marc brought to the table that I liked because he just got so much enjoyment out of them. Ninety per cent of the non-sports stuff: redheads, nudity, anything that had nothing to do with sport, were Marc's ideas.

I loved getting my mates on the show doing absurd things. Half the giggle was seeing if they would pull it off, if the people sitting at home would believe it. I'd say to Ric, 'What do you want? How about a possum skinner, a tree climber, or an axe thrower?' Then I'd get one of the boys to chuck on some gear that was relevant — a pair of adidas tracksuit pants or a harness — and come on.

The Human Cannonball was Ben Hickey, one of my greatest mates. We had caused a lot of trouble together at varsity. Ric went along with the idea and Ben pretended that his goal was to be fired over the Sydney Harbour Bridge at the opening of the Olympic Games. Waffle came on as his trainer. Cannonball was so convincing, with his deadpan look, his description of being blown out of his cannon, and his mantra, 'Hard and erect, hard and erect', that he ended up being a permanent part of the show. He travelled around a lot — to the Hong Kong Sevens and over to the Olympics with the Kiwi team. He was involved in the America's Cup kerfuffle. In the end, though, the temptations that come with that sort of exposure became a bit much for him and he had to call it quits and return to the real world.

That Guy, a.k.a. Leigh Hart, was a mate from varsity too. He was just one of those guys I knew would be really, really funny, and he turned out to be even funnier than I thought. Initially, he came on as a professional snail racer. He had the old adidas tracksuit on and a two-litre ice-cream container full of snails from my garden. He picked each snail out of the bucket and explained what it was called. Then he took his shoe off and crushed one, claiming it was lame. It was a command performance and he did a superb job.

He was such a natural that he became That Guy, our roving reporter, and he did some hellishly amusing stuff. It must have been quite a challenge to come up with something new and unique every week for the years he was on 'Sports Café', but he had the ability to be very creative. I liked his cooking segments, when he'd smash the window to get into his flat, then just throw eggs, flour, you name it, in the blender and around his kitchen. Speedo cops and yeti-hunting were brilliant too. He's since gone on to carve his own sort of space in New Zealand TV, with his show 'Moon TV'. He is as good as Billy T. James or Fred Dagg I reckon, and I'd love to see him on primetime.

Of all the characters we had on the show, Ralph was my favourite. On our 100th show I said to Ric, 'Hey, we need a gimp'. Ric said, 'No. I've got an eight-year-old kid and I don't want to have to try to explain to him when he watches the show at home what this is all about.' I said, 'You're the father and that's going to be your challenge, because we're getting a gimp'.

I recruited the services of a friend (who shall remain nameless) and we based Ralph on the gimp in 'Pulp Fiction'. We went to the Den, an adult store in Auckland, and got him the suit, and then we shot off and filmed him dragging a conger eel through the middle of Newmarket. He was perfect, born for that suit. He had such freedom of movement: he walked and danced just like a gimp should.

Ralph had said right from the start that he would only do the show if his anonymity was assured, and for the most part he stayed anonymous. But I made the mistake of telling my dad who Ralph really was, and to watch the show the first night he was on. My old man is top mates with Ralph's old man, and was so excited he called Ralph Senior and told him to watch 'Sports Café'. Ralph's dancing was so distinctive that, first night on the show, his cover was blown with his parents. I was not popular.

Ric Salizzo: The thing that was funny about Ralph was that Marc thought it was so funny. I didn't think it was anywhere near as funny as Marc did. It's fair to say it was the subject of a lot of arguments between Marc and myself.

Ric didn't understand Ralph, but he understood that other people liked him. The aim with Ralph was to put him in completely inappropriate situations. We'd take him along to the beach and make him dive off the wharf; we filmed him dragging a cooked Peking duck on a dog chain through town and tossing it off a flyover onto a railway track. (That got us in trouble with the Ministry of Transport.) He'd pop up from behind the couch on the show and start mumbling at guests. At the America's Cup parade, we jumped on the end of it and I drove Ralph up Queen Street on a Vespa. He was waving to the crowds. People were quite surprised to see him in the parade. When we got to the top of Queen Street I chucked him off and he had to make his way down to the bottom of Queen Street dressed as a gimp. Rather than walk down normally he slunk his way down, mumbling to himself and nodding his head. A few people came up and asked for his autograph and, apparently, he signed, 'Spank Me, Ralph'.

* * *

The first hot water I got myself into was with the infamous 'sweating like a rapist' comment. We had the trans-Atlantic rowers, Rob Hamill and Phil Stubbs, on the show. I made the comment that as it had been so hot out there, they must have been 'sweating like a rapist'. I meant of course (because I'm not a complete moron), sweating like a rapist waiting for the long arm of the law to come and collar him. Not sweating like a rapist in the act.

I don't mind being a stirrer; in fact I quite enjoy it. But often I don't go out of my way to stir anyone; it just happens. In this case, what I said was a bit tongue in cheek, said for a bit of a dag, and it got blown out of proportion. It *really* didn't go down well.

Ric Salizzo: I learnt very early on that when it came to defending Marc in the press, which I've had to do fairly regularly, I had to be very careful. On the 'sweating like a rapist' show I apologised 19 times within 30 seconds of him saying it. I knew exactly what he meant, but I also knew how it would be interpreted. In those situations you can't get too bogged down with who's right and who's wrong. You have to think about how people are going to react, and I knew how people were going to react.

Rape Crisis got up in arms. They claimed I was belittling victims of rape and making light of a very serious subject. I'd have to be totally emotionally bereft, a vile piece of work, to have meant to do that. If I'd meant it like that I could see it would have been a despicable thing to do, but I was just using a turn of phrase; it was a saying that was going around, admittedly a fairly non-PC one. I possibly shouldn't have said it, but some people interpreted it wrongly and blew it out of proportion.

Ric Salizzo: The next day Rape Crisis made a statement in the papers. Sky left it up to me to resolve. I rang Rape Crisis and had a chat and explained the whole context and what he meant. The woman said that she appreciated that but it was too good an opportunity to get publicity. In their eyes he overstepped the mark and that gave them the opportunity to get publicity out of it. Marc, like a lot of competitive people, gets defensive in those situations. He thinks, 'I'm not going to let them beat me'. But in that situation it was better to apologise and get on with it.

Speaking of exposure, we caused a bit of a fuss with Nude Day too. As I've mentioned before, I've always championed any opportunity to get nude. I thought that by introducing the idea on 'Sports Café' we had the potential to take it nationwide. Ric loved it the moment it was mentioned, so we really got behind it. The theory was to set up one day a year when people could get their kit off and express themselves in their God-given form.

We asked people to send in tapes of themselves doing bizarre things in the nick. I got the ball rolling with a nude lawn-mowing and bacon-frying skit. (Another year I went to Auckland Zoo naked with a T-bone steak strapped to my groin, but the zoo officials caught me dropping my tweeds outside the lion's cage, decided it wasn't right, and took the tape from me.) We had some funny characters that first year and more than a few that couldn't go to air. The concept was especially embraced by the rural community and the winner was a guy who came out of the bush nude, with a knife strapped to him and a pig on his shoulders. Nude pig-hunting. Brilliant.

We celebrated the first Nude Day with a party at Leftfield in Auckland. Naturally, one had to be nude to get in and we organised spa pools and free booze. We had about a hundred people nude, just cruising around upstairs. Of course, it all turned pear-shaped about 11 p.m., once everyone had had a bit to drink. There was a little heavy petting in the spa pool by a couple from Waiheke Island, but things came right once they got on the ferry home.

Nude Day wasn't a sexual thing, just a sort of anti-establishment bit of light-hearted fun. And it was something that became a part of the show and was looked forward to immensely. Over the years we had some really, really funny entries. Some of the stuff couldn't even be shown on TV. (Guy from Invercargill, you know who you are.) I would so look forward to going into the office to watch the latest Nude Day entries when that time of the year came around. There were farmers tearing around on their motorbikes in the nude; guys in the nude getting dragged behind cars on sacks; guys walking into lectures nude; and people in the nude surfing with seals down on Stewart Island. We had a couple of policemen from down south jump out of a police car nude (sadly, they got fired for that); a nude fire brigade, putting out a car on fire; people going through car washes strapped to the roof, in the nude; and nude fire-walking. One guy even got a bike parked up his nude arse-crack.

It took a couple of years before the ladies got in on it, but when they did, it was a fine day indeed. Helen Clark was the only person who I insisted stay clothed. I thought it was in the best interests of the general public, and Helen herself, to be frank. She never commented on the ban, but it would have been great had she done so. As it turned out, she sent a message to us for the last show, and made a few cracks, which showed she has a good sense of humour and suggested she may have seen the odd show.

In recent years I asked viewers to streak during NPC games, to film it and send it in and we'd reward them with $1000 (per security guard they could elude). Female streakers were promised a washing machine and an ironing board. It didn't quite have the pulling power of cash, so I later changed it to $2000 for the women.

There were streakers all the time when I was playing rugby in Dunedin. In 1993 there was a spate of them. We were playing a game, an intense game, and this nude guy suddenly jumped the fence and ran onto the field. He came sprinting straight towards me. I thought, 'I recognise that blonde afro', and I did — it was my flatmate Woody! In the court session I had to explain why a nude man had run straight for me in the middle of the game and had to have a few beers for my flatmate. I thought it was priceless.

Viewers took up the streaking challenge and started sending in clips of themselves. A number of them got arrested, which I thought ridiculous. Our friends from After Birth Productions (they entered every competition we put up) sent in a streak filmed in Taranaki. On the tape you'd hear the roar of the crowd every time this guy got past a security guard.

There was an outcry about the whole thing. The talkback nuts jumped on the bandwagon, calling up radio stations and saying, 'I'll never buy Charlie's products again because Marc Ellis is condoning nudity'. I agreed to have a chat on Radio Rhema and was hijacked by the religious right. People were calling up saying that streaking was offensive to children. My argument was that what was more offensive to children was a religious zealot standing on a soapbox telling people that they were going to burn in hell if they didn't subscribe to a religious doctrine. That went down particularly poorly.

Eventually, I had to go on the 'Holmes' show to debate the issue. There was someone else on, I can't remember who, who claimed it was offensive behaviour. I said that the NZRU and everybody else should just relax. I've never known anybody go to the rugby or the cricket and see a streaker and yell, 'Boo!' It's seen as a fun thing, a great laugh. It gives folks something to have a chat about in the pub afterwards. The only booing that occurs is when a security guard takes it too seriously and takes the streaker's head off. The NPC was boring, they were having record low attendances that year, and lightening it up by getting people to sprint onto the fields and beat security guards could only improve it.

The debate continues. I was driving back from Piha recently and I heard Murray Deaker chastising streakers on his radio show. Some poor woman had done a streak in the weekend and been knocked unconscious by an over zealous security buffoon. Murray said she deserved it so I called talkback for the first time in my life.

* * *

The night I was drunk on air I really got into trouble. That season the show had been pushed back from 8.30 p.m. to 9.30 p.m. I'd gone out for a business lunch this particular Wednesday and we'd ended up having a few red wines. I bumped into another couple of mates later on and by 9.30 p.m. we'd had a few more red wines *and* a few tequilas. By the time I got to the show I was in a very happy place, but I was not in a place where I was going to make any coherent sense at all.

Ric Salizzo: I was genuinely angry with Marc that night. That was the angriest he's ever made me. He turned up late as usual, but pretty close to our on-air time. We were sitting down ready to start the show when he showed up and I didn't quite realise how bad he was. I thought he might have been winding me up, putting it on, but five minutes into the show I realised he couldn't talk. I wanted to kill him. What irritated me the most was that we had a really great line-up of guests — Richie Barnett, Daryl Halligan and others — and Marc was stuffing up the show. I could see the whole show just crumbling. Everyone else loved it — the audience, everyone else.

I recall Ric saying, 'For Christ's sake, you're really going to have to pull your socks up in the second half'. There wasn't much chance of that happening.

Ric Salizzo: After the first break I kicked him off the show, told him to go and get some coffee. We had a big fibreglass cow on the set, so I put that in his place, so in

192

Quite possibly my greatest moment in sport — the world cheese-rolling championships, Gloucestershire, 2004.

Party in Melbourne with Dave and Agustina.

Someone found some tequila . . . and this became Bruce's last photo.

My mate 'The Walrus' prepares for some speed skating.

Shucking scallops for the barbecue . . . it's very hard to beat a summer at the beach.

The perfect dinner — scallops, crayfish and cocktails.

Darts and pool of an evening . . .

The Ginger Camel and Johnny the Greek.

The Tongan Yam — legend of the Castle Street Mile.

The summer racing carnival in Auckland brings out the worst people.

My mate's wedding in Spain featured the 'Great Spanish Pipe-off', including the great Sir Ed.

Hadge and me proudly perched on our respective Valiants.

The old uni crew gathered from around the world for a mate's wedding on Waiheke Island.

Same crew as above — this time in Thailand at another wedding.

It was a great moment.

Agustina and I with the entire wedding party . . . and below with our proud parents.

Now all in their mid-30s, the southern university representatives have had it all over their northern counterparts for the past decade, both on and off the pitch.

Southern — winners of the Auckland Business House cricket competition for three years running. This is as close to competitive sport as I get these days.

the wide shots there wouldn't be a hole. Coming back from the commercial break he snuck on and started arguing with the cow.

The highlight, or rather, lowlight, came when I went to demonstrate a kicking technique and booted a rugby ball straight at the face of a woman sitting in the audience. It skimmed off the top of her head and gave her an awful fright. That drew gasps from the crowd. And I started laughing because I thought it was hilarious.

I felt very bad the next day (and quite hung over). I phoned Ric and apologised and admitted that I knew I'd crossed the line. He copped a lot of flak from the network, so the official word on it was that I was acting. I was — I was trying to act sober.

The next big controversy was the America's Cup break-in. 'Sports Café' had put together an entrant for the Cup, a piss-take. It was a raft that we built and named Team Bulgaria, and moored outside Leftfield. Eva was the patron of our team.

One week Ric asked us to do a skit with Team Bulgaria, so Ralph, the Cannonball, a cameraman and I decided to try to get into one of the bases. The Cannonball dressed in his suit and Ralph dressed up as the gimp. We all put balaclavas on and a bit of chalk on our faces. We shot off underneath the wharves in this little duck-shooting boat a viewer had lent us, then turned the engine off because it was making too much noise and rowed past the surveillance boats and the security. When we got into the America True base we climbed out of the boat and put glasses against the keel of the boat, as if we were listening to what was going on. Ralph was rolling about in their sails, while the Human Cannonball was tearing around the place calling out, 'Hard and erect, hard and erect!'. Sure enough, it wasn't long before all the lights came on and the security guards came tearing around the corner. It really turned pear-shaped. We were lucky to get out of there without getting arrested.

Ric Salizzo: I came into work the next morning to a number of irate phone calls and one from Marc saying that we were 'in the shit'. America True was genuinely angry. They talked about suing us. They just couldn't understand what was going on: Marc, along with a gimp and a human cannonball, breaking into their base for no good reason. They took all the footage the guys had filmed and we had to agree not to air any of it. The police got involved. The Government was annoyed with us. They felt they'd gone to all this trouble to host the event and idiots like Marc undermined the security. It made all the papers and the TV. I was told not to make light of it on the show.

It was just a bit of fun, but they didn't see any humour in it. So we had no choice but to make a formal apology to America True. How you can take a guy dressed in a wetsuit and a balaclava, accompanied by a gimp and a guy in a human cannonball outfit seriously, I don't know, but I guess they had to make an example of anyone caught on the base. Ric was pretty annoyed. But by the time the next week's show rolled around, he could see the funny side. And he let us make our apology in Bulgarian. I read it out and the Cannonball 'interpreted' it — 'There's been a travesty of justice for which we are partly responsible' it began. Then Ralph stepped forward and got 10 whacks on the arse with a boat paddle from Eva. That was our official apology.

I don't know whether 'Sports Café' got any better or any worse over the years, but the last year of the show it rated higher than ever. I loved it, loved doing it, the live aspect of it, the interaction with the guests, having a few beers and a yarn. It was the only show I know of where the hosts are paid to turn up, sit down with their mates, have a bit of a yarn, and be as big a nuisance as possible. It was just perfect for me. But after 10 years Ric decided to knock it on the head and I respect that. Most TV producers don't choose to end a show — they wait until it gets canned. It would have been very easy for all of us to keep going season after season, but Ric said, 'That's enough now, time for a new challenge'. It was the right thing to do, and I love that we went out that way.

Serious Trouble

W hen I was a kid my old man used to say, 'If it feels good and it's not hurting anyone, do it'. It's a pretty good philosophy and one I've subscribed to for the most part, and I've gone out of my way to ensure that I have a life that's included a lot of fun, and that I haven't hurt anyone in the process. In 2005, however, I took that idea too literally and it led to serious trouble.

I was in London filming a new series of 'Rocky Road' with Ridgey when we got a call from Julie Christie. She said there was talk I had been implicated in a drug ring in Auckland. That was all she knew — that me and a few other characters had been implicated, but I knew immediately what the scenario was and what I had been caught doing.

Julie Christie: I was called up by someone at TVNZ and told that Matthew and Marc were going to appear in court. I said, 'How can that be possible?'. I ignored it. Then, of course, two days later, it all came out. To tell you the truth, I didn't believe it. I didn't even ask him if he did it. But by the second phone call with Marc, he sounded resigned, like he knew he'd done something wrong.

The first thing I did after hearing from Julie was to call my folks, which was a pretty tough thing to do. I explained to them that I'd been implicated in a drug bust and understood that the police had details of me buying drugs. They were my primary concern. I'd let them down. I'd been brought up well, to lead a good life and to have high standards, and now I was hearing my dad's voice break on the phone. It was awful.

They were really, really supportive, but it wasn't easy for them to understand what Ecstasy is and why I'd tried it.

Chris Ellis: It was bad news. He'd messed up, literally. And it was hard to deal with because Marc was away overseas. We were under a lot of stress. But we wanted to support Marc.

Julie Christie: Was I surprised it was true? No, I guess I wasn't. We weren't talking about P or heroin or anything.

At that stage I didn't know exactly what the police had or what the charges were. Name suppression had been imposed by the court, but that lasted a blink of an eye. The media weren't allowed to report on the case, but they told their mates, and word got around. New Zealand's too small for it not to. I hadn't even been charged with anything, but the whole country was talking about it.

Ric Salizzo: That certainly showed that the suppression laws in New Zealand are a joke. If you have name suppression, you should get name suppression. The judge decided that and it should have been suppressed. Marc hadn't even been charged with anything and everyone was talking about it.

There was no real point in coming back early, so I stayed and did the work that I'd been contracted to do for 'Rocky Road'. Ridgey and I and the crew went on to Russia. I told myself that until I had the facts there was no point worrying about it, but that was easier said than done. While I tried to be as chipper as ever, it was actually bloody difficult to keep my chin up.

Matthew Ridge: It really rocked him. And me too. We were both more than concerned. We knew the drama that would be going on at home. He was upset for himself, but also his family and people who knew him. He felt he'd let people down and was worried about his future.

I knew the pain that my parents would be going through and that hurt. I was nervous about how it would all be interpreted by everyone. Every now and then Ridgey and I would find an Internet café and go online to read the New Zealand papers. There was plenty of speculation and conjecture in New Zealand chat rooms: people saying that they knew I was a druggie, because of the way I behaved on TV. It was all bullshit and I tried to have a laugh at those sorts of things.

Matthew Ridge: Normally, it's me they're pinning shit on. We'd joked about that in the past. Marc's far from a goodie two-shoes, but he's the Teflon kid — nothing sticks.

I was in constant contact with my dad, my lawyer, and with mates like Ric Salizzo who were keeping me up to date with what was happening.

Ric Salizzo: I was worried for him. I was worried that he wouldn't get through it. I was worried about how serious the charges might be and how far they might push it. It was a horrible time. I hated it, particularly those first couple of weeks, while Marc was away, when nobody knew what was going on.

In hindsight I think it was good that I was overseas when the story broke. I could stay out of the spotlight while my father organised a lawyer, the late Robert Fardell QC, who went with Dad to the police. And I avoided the hundreds of calls from the media.

Matthew Ridge: We had time to collect our thoughts. It was hard getting information from people, but as more and more came in we realised what the police had. We went through highs and lows really. One night I woke up and he was talking to his dad. He went into the bathroom and broke down. It was a really hard time. And as a mate it was hard too. Everyone's done something wrong. It was illegal, but it wasn't like Marc hurt anybody.

On the other hand, the media had six weeks to turn the whole thing into a frenzy, a 'celebrity drug bust'. Because of that and my high profile I feared I wouldn't be let off. Some of that shit, because of the media beat-up, had to stick. The police were stuck between a rock and a hard place and despite telling my lawyer that they usually wouldn't bother with a mere possession charge, particularly with a first offender, they now had to follow it through to the nth degree. I hadn't murdered anyone; I hadn't beaten anyone up or stolen anything; but I was guilty of buying an illegal drug and I had screwed up.

I've experimented with drugs pretty much as any other young person of my age has, but with one difference: I didn't finish playing sport until I was 30. I was involved in professional sport when a number of my associates were dabbling. I couldn't — and nor for that matter did I want to — have any real relationship with drugs. Players were drug-tested and, besides, I didn't want my performance on the field to be affected. I'd have a few beers after a game and that would do me. That was lucky, I think; it allowed me to experiment mostly when I was in my 30s and more level-headed. When I finished sport I could look at the people around me and understand from their experience what the ramifications of trying drugs were.

The first drug I tried was marijuana, when I was 16. I was on a summer holiday, a road-trip, with three mates. We stopped to set up camp somewhere near Gisborne and one of the boys pulled out a joint. It was a beautiful day and the perfect opportunity to try it. After we smoked it, it took us about two hours to put the tent up and we rolled around with laughter. It was a great, light-hearted experience with friends. To me, that's not an abhorrent act and it happens often all over New Zealand in all sorts of social situations. (According to the New Zealand Drug Foundation 50 per cent of all New Zealanders have tried cannabis.)

Marijuana was fairly prevalent at varsity but, as I say, I couldn't partake most of the year. Every now and then in the holidays, when I wasn't going to be drug-tested, I might have had a joint, though I would never pay for it. I drew the line at buying.

I inadvertently tried 'magic mushrooms' once too, while I was at varsity. By the time I realised what was in the tea I'd been given it was too late, I was half gone. Before long, three of us were off. We were climbing up onto our flatmate's wardrobe and jumping onto her bed, which had a blue duvet on it, because we thought it was a swimming pool. We had rainbows coming out of our hands. I fell in love with a girl on a *Cleo* cover. Eventually we went to the pub and drank like fishes.

I woke up the next morning and should have felt a lot worse than I did. I had a rugby game and I played one of the best games I've ever played, probably because I was so nervous the drugs would affect my play. I had had a fun night, because I was with three really good mates, but it wasn't for me. And I didn't try mushrooms again.

On 25 June 2005 I was at a party in Auckland. The All Blacks had just played against the Lions in Christchurch and we'd had a couple of beers and watched the game. We were in high spirits, and with a few drinks onboard another person and I made the foolish decision to go and buy a couple of Ecstasy pills. The net result was that I had a big smile on my face for a few hours and cut a few shapes on the dance floor. The rest, as they say, is history, and the price I paid well documented.

The day I flew home to New Zealand to face the music the media figured out what flight I was on, so they were all waiting at Auckland airport. I was stopped at immigration and all my bags were rifled through with a fine-tooth comb. My old man was there to pick me up and he took me home, where photographers were camped out on the street. I was ready for it because I'd psyched myself up, but it was all quite disconcerting, and I knew this was the start of a fairly ordinary chapter in my life.

Chris Ellis: And so Marc came back and he was pretty worried about meeting with the police. That must have been very difficult, that discussion.

That afternoon I sat down with my lawyer, ascertained what the police had against me, and booked a meeting with them. I had wanted to see the police straight away — I was keen to get in there and tell the truth and get it all out in the open — but they couldn't see me for four days because of a big trial they were working on. I spent the next four days being stalked by the bloody paparazzi, in little old New Zealand, for God's sake: I'd go to the gym, or to work in the morning, and guys would jump out of cars and start snapping photos.

On 26 August I finally got to sit down with the police. The policemen were friendly, nice guys. I co-operated with them fully. I admitted I bought the drugs, I offered to go to court straight away.

By that stage the police were discussing prosecuting me for conspiracy to supply. I had mentioned a few other names when buying the drugs, which meant I could be done for conspiracy. Once I explained why I had mentioned other people they accepted that, but said they would have to charge me for possession. Even though it was my first offence, I would have to be convicted. I accepted that; after all, I had done something illegal and I should have had to pay the price for that.

I was dressed in an open-collared shirt that day, so I asked if I could swing by home to put on a suit before I went to court. The police allowed me to do that, which was good of them. I believe the police are good dudes. I have always had a healthy respect for the police, and despite what happened, will continue to do so. I think they do a great job, sometimes under very trying circumstances, and I think they're special folk.

I was taken to the holding cells under the courthouse. A few people thought it was a bit average that I was put in the holding cells. It wasn't as if I was a flight risk at that stage — everyone knew what I'd done and I'd admitted it to the police, and I certainly wasn't a danger to society, but it didn't really bother me. In fact, the experience was highly amusing. I was there for about three hours and they turned out to be some of the most interesting hours of my life.

I was put in my own cell, which was probably just as well as one of the guys down the hallway voiced an interest in a sexual relationship with me (by way of a very explicit eight-word sentence). I guess that's a compliment of sorts. I chatted to the other guys down there. There were some real characters. They'd lived really colourful lives. I asked them what jail was like; they told me it was better than being out on the streets. They had everything they needed in jail, they said, including most of their mates.

At lunchtime my cellmates started whingeing for fish and chips and banging on the bars. The police went out and got them salad sandwiches and bought fish and chips for themselves, which I thought was classic. The same chap who had voiced his interest in a brief physical relationship with me was beside himself when he didn't get his greasies. I wound him up by calling one of the guards over for a chat. When he left I thanked him loudly for the milkshake and hot chips. The game worked — my love interest flew into a rage and gave us the most impressive display of cagework I've ever witnessed!

Sometime after lunch I was brought up to the courtroom and put in the dock. It's all a bit of a blur now, but I remember my head was hanging pretty damn low at that stage. I'd asked my dad and Agustina to stay out of the courtroom because I didn't want to look out and see them there — I would have got a little mist on for sure. I pleaded guilty to possession of a Class B drug and was convicted under the Misuse of Drugs Act and fined $300 plus court costs.

I came out and made a statement to the media, apologising to my family and friends. I knew exactly what I wanted to say and I didn't want to be too over the top, just say a few words and then push off. I wanted to apologise to my folks and to those who were close to me because, regardless of what anyone else thought, I felt responsible for my family and friends. I felt like I had damaged my family name.

Chris Ellis: It was the first time anyone in the Ellis family had had a criminal conviction.

Ric Salizzo: I thought Marc handled himself really well outside the court. He had let people down — his family and friends — by being in that situation. But, everyone makes mistakes. And he admitted his.

Julie Christie: When he stood outside the court you could see how genuinely devastated he was. He handled it brilliantly. He apologised to his family and that went down well — New Zealanders like family.

I wanted to make one statement and one statement only. People can see if you're genuine or not and I was genuinely gutted. You don't need to say too much to get that point across. Afterwards, there were offers to sell the story to various newspapers and magazines, but that didn't interest me. I had screwed up and come clean, and I just wanted to get on with other things. The media have a knack of hanging you with your own rope if you talk too much.

I felt awkward apologising to my supporters — who am I to believe that I've got supporters? — but Ric explained that I should thank the people I didn't know who were rooting for me. He was right, because it later transpired, when letters and emails started arriving, that a lot of New Zealanders were behind me.

Chris Ellis: Friends were very supportive. In the first three or four days we'd had a number of phone calls from people saying they were thinking of us. It takes quite a lot of gumption to ring up a family and say that in those circumstances. I kept a list over the following days of people thoughtful enough to get in touch. The list grew and grew and grew. That meant a great deal to the family.

My next stop was an emergency board meeting at Charlie's. Simon and Stefan had been under a fair bit of pressure at work since the story had been leaked, and were naturally worried about the effect it would have on the business. I was too, and in the board meeting I told them what had happened. I explained that I was proud of who I was, but that I also knew I had to step down from the board. It was the right thing to do. We had a really good board and if Charlie's wanted to retain the services of board members like Ted van Arkel, the former head of Progressive, I had to go. Those men were well-respected businessmen and would have been compromised by me remaining on the board. I didn't want their names tarnished by my mistake. It was best to stand down and let the Charlie's consumers dictate what kind of penalty I'd pay, and then I could make a decision based on what that reception was down the line. It was incredibly difficult and I had tears in my eyes when I said I was stepping down. The guys could see how much Charlie's meant to me.

Stefan Lepionka: If he had wanted to stay, we would have supported that, and when he wanted to leave, we supported that too. I cried in that meeting. It felt like the end of an era. It was really, really difficult.

The media jumped on my resignation and said Charlie's' share price took a hammering because of my conviction. The truth is Charlie's had issued warrants (to raise capital) at 10 cents, which naturally pulled the share price down to 10 cents per share. That just happened to occur at the same time as my drug conviction and any journalist worth their salt would have done their research and figured that out, but it made a better story to say the drop was down to me.

That afternoon I got a call from Marcus Foot, owner of HRV Ventilation, a company for which I had done an advertising campaign. He phoned and explained HRV was sticking by me and that was a huge boost of confidence — I can't even explain what a boost it was. In a really bad time, on such an awful day, to have somebody support you, rather than condemn you, meant a lot.

That night Ric went on 'Close Up' with Susan Wood to speak for me. I was pleased that she'd asked Ric to go on her show rather than get someone — an anti-drug campaigner or suchlike — who would use my predicament for political advantage or free publicity. I got home in time to watch it that night and I thought Ric did a superb job, as he always does. He has such a level head and is very good at summarising public opinion and he just handled it really well.

Ric Salizzo: I didn't want to be interviewed by Susan Wood. I didn't want to be involved (because I prefer to be in the background), but it was better than Marc doing it. Marc's initial response is always to come out fighting, which I understand — I'm exactly the same when I'm cornered. But sometimes you have to fight with a bit more strategy.

All of my other mates were really, really supportive too. I think I'm a good judge of character and if you are my friend it's not by accident — it's because I love your company and because you're loyal. And all my friends definitely proved that throughout the whole experience.

Repercussions

Ifelt like I was in a fairly precarious position immediately after my conviction. I had given the people who disliked me a real reason to. On the other hand, those people who liked me seemed to have more empathy with me. For a wee while I would constantly try to gauge how people responded to me. I'd be yarning to people and trying to read between the lines to see what they thought of me. I was worried about how people in the business community, people my parents' age, would take it. Would they see it for what it was? Or would they see it as something reprehensible? Turns out they've been really forgiving. People could see I was hurting, having to step down from the company I started.

It's amazing in New Zealand — when you're up, there's an element that want to bring you down. And when you're down, people want to help you out. Once I'd fronted up to everything and been to court I got an amazing amount of support from the general public. About 300 emails were sent to me via the Charlie's website, 'Sports Café', and Touchdown Productions, all from people I didn't know, and along the following lines:

Mr Ellis, Chin up mate, we all make mistakes, and most of us don't get caught while we're making them . . .

Hi Marc, I just thought I would send you an email to say that I am behind you 100% and am sending you my support from London … There are far more serious things going on in this world that we should be looking at. Just because you are of a certain status, the whole country will possibly be looking at you in a different light. Keep strong, kia kaha, there are a lot of us out there who are behind you and want to support you . . .

I'd like to express my deep concern at the recent acceptance of the resignation of Marc Ellis from the board of Charlie's. I have been a supporter of your products for the past couple of years (great products indeed) but would like to protest Mr Ellis's resignation by no longer supporting your product range. I have spoken with a number of friends since this unfortunate PC decision and I can inform you I am far from alone in my stand.

I am a mother and a grandmother on the wrong side of 60 and it would be fair to say I am pretty representative of middle New Zealand. I love your humour and talent, which has turned many a dull evening into something quite special for a lot of us. The unfortunate events of last week are seen by most people that I speak to as exactly what they are — a bad choice at the time, but pretty minor in the general scheme of things . . .

Ninety per cent of communications I got were positive. Charlie's received a number of emails from people who wouldn't buy its products any more because the company had accepted my resignation from the board. That probably gave the guys confidence that the brand wouldn't suffer as a result of me having done something silly. There were only a few from shoppers who would no longer buy Charlie's:

I think it is very damaging to your company that Marc Ellis has been convicted. What sort of a role model is he providing? Myself and my family will never buy your product again for this reason. There are plenty of other quality juice brands without bad reputations.

It was overwhelming really, that people went out of their way to write. I was quite choked up by it and I replied to every message.

I was very fortunate to keep my TV jobs. Julie and Ric had been talking to TVNZ while I was away and on my return I kept the management of TVNZ — which screens 'Sports Café', 'Game of Two Halves' and 'Rocky Road' — informed. I was thrilled that I didn't have to pull out of my TV work. I'd already had to step down from Charlie's, so to lose that as well would have been a huge kick in the guts, particularly given the effort I'd put into TV over the previous 10 years. I think the television industry is probably more realistic about the social realities than many other industries and I was hugely appreciative of the support I got from TVNZ, Julie and Ric. It was cool that they stuck by me.

Ric Salizzo: The first thing I had to think about was what was best for 'Sports Café', then what was best for me, then what was best for Marc. It was pretty obvious that the show was better with him there. And I thought it was best for Marc that he was on the show. So long as he handled himself well through all this, there was never any danger of him leaving. If he'd acted poorly, it would have been hard to keep him on the show. It blew over because he fronted up and took it on the chin and then got on with things.

Julie Christie: TVNZ were brilliant. Never once did they suggest cancelling shows or anything.

I wondered whether I should take a few weeks off 'Sports Café' to keep a low profile, but Ric believed I should come back on with a smile and move on. We had a meeting and agreed we would steer well clear of any reference or innuendo about my conviction.

About 10 minutes before the first show we met the guests. One was former Wallaby prop Dan Crowley, who was on the show to promote his new book, *Undercover*. No one had checked the title or the contents of the book. As the name suggests, it was about Dan going undercover to bust drug rings on Queensland's Gold Coast. In the end he came on and said, 'I've got a new book out'. That was all he could say. We all had a laugh at the timing of that one.

One day I came in to TVNZ to tell management where I was at. It was before my appointment with the police and I wanted to make sure TVNZ knew I was taking it all very seriously. I knew the media would be on the lookout for me and I managed to get in the front door of the building without being seen. But it wasn't long before some woman with a camera, a 'One News' reporter, started chasing me.

She kept asking over and over if I had a drug problem, which I thought was a bit low. She had sprung me at one of my places of work and was going down the road of that typical sensationalist line of questioning. Of course I don't have a drug problem. If I did there'd be no way in the world I'd be able to hold down my job at Charlie's doing 50 hours a week, keep fit and in a relationship, and do the TV stuff I do on the side. It was a ludicrous question, and she knew it. Naturally, I refused to dignify her question with an answer. I was annoyed that TVNZ played the footage from that encounter days later, after I'd been to court.

Julie Christie: That was filmed on the Monday. There were four cameras waiting for us. It was appalling, but that's just the way they are. It was silly. They showed it as if it was the day he went to court. I made an official complaint and they upheld it.

On the whole, though, I've got no gripe with the media or how they handled the whole thing. I can't do anything about the media, so there's no point getting angry about it. New Zealand's a small country and there isn't a lot of news so I understand that the media had to jump on it. Some did a better job than others, some had an agenda to push, but really they were just doing their jobs. To hear Judy Bailey call me a 'convicted drug felon' on national TV was hard, but it wasn't the end of the world. To call it a 'celebrity drug bust' when I was the only guy collared is a bit of an exaggeration, but that's OK.

Possibly the media's take on the whole thing actually encouraged public sympathy. Soon after my conviction I was nominated for Personality of the Year at the Qantas Media Awards. I'm not really interested in accolades for my TV stuff, but to be nominated for that was quite cool, and to win it — to get that vote of confidence from the public at that time of my life — was really cool. I felt like people were rooting for me.

Julie Christie: The New Zealand public were saying that he'd handled himself really well and that they didn't care.

One thing I was lambasted for was being a poor role model. I find that disappointing and hard to accept. I've never professed to be a role model for kids; I've never stuck myself on a pedestal, or claimed to be perfect. I'm far from perfect and I concede that openly. There's only one way to go if you think you're perfect and that's down. So when I hear some rooster on the radio clucking away about how I've set a bad example to the kids that look up to me, I think that's unfair.

My parents were my role models and that's how it should be. When I am a parent I hope my children will see me as a good role model, but I think that if a child has to grow up looking at someone like me for guidance, rather than their own family, that's a real problem. Making me a role model creates a responsibility, an expectation that I'll behave in a certain manner. I haven't asked for that and I've never pretended to be anyone other than who I am. I'm not a politically correct person and I'm not appropriate all of the time. I make mistakes. And I'll make more mistakes. That's the sort of person I am. I've learnt from this whole experience, however, that the more people who know who you are, the more careful you have to be. I have a natural predisposition to worrying about how I am perceived. When I come in after a night out, I often get the demons and wonder if I've upset anyone or gone too far.

There's not a place in New Zealand that I haven't got carried away in at one time or another and generally people don't mind me having a good time. They expect me to be a bit loose. I love to have a few drinks and get up to shenanigans and I'm a happy drunk. I never get into fights, but I get cuddly and love to throw hongis around, so it's pretty hard to misinterpret that sort of behaviour. And I've always been myself. I always wanted to be the same guy I've always been, believing that if I got to the stage where I didn't do something just because I'm a public figure, I'd be a bit of a wanker. I've realised that that isn't the best attitude for someone living under a spotlight. I need to watch myself a bit.

There's always someone waiting for me to cock up and sadly I have to be more mindful of that. Two months after my conviction I went to the cricket at Eden Park. I had a great day with my mates in a friend's private box. At the end of the day we stripped off to our underwear, just for shits and giggles. And it made the papers.

Another case in point was my stag do. I intentionally had it on a Sunday and out of Auckland. I knew that if I had it in the middle of Auckland, on a Friday or Saturday night, chances were the media would get wind of it and make a story out of nothing. So my mates hired a private venue, the Waiheke Island Bowling Club, and we had a great day there. On the ferry ride home it was alleged — I missed all this because I was having a lie-down — one or two of the guys behaved badly. Even though I wasn't one of those people, the journalists started phoning. It was turned into a story and I was implicated; my photo was put in the paper and I was accused of 'late-night drunken mayhem'. I'd expect that from a paper like *Truth*, but this was the *National Business Review*.

The most disappointing feedback I got over the whole drugs affair was from people excusing my conviction by saying, 'Oh well, he does live that lifestyle' or 'He is under a lot of pressure'. That's bullshit. What happened to me hasn't got anything to do with my lifestyle, or how hard I work, or the mates I hang out with. I'm not someone who goes to the opening of things on a regular basis. I don't go to social events around town where you get seen and your photo gets taken for the newspapers. That's not me. The public perception of people being in a position where they do that kind of thing doesn't interest me.

The fact is that drugs use is prevalent among my generation. They are much more mainstream than in the past. Having said that, I personally believe it's in everyone's interests for drugs to be illegal. Drugs are a complicated issue and any argument for or against is complicated too.

I have heard of many New Zealand families that have been destroyed by drug abuse and that's terrible. If you legalise drugs, and the one most often talked about in this regard is cannabis — probably because it's the most widely used illegal drug — I think the people who are inclined to be lost to it will be lost much quicker. The catchment of people who could be lost to it will broaden. Cannabis is not a drug that will necessarily kill you, but if used on a daily basis, it will have a detrimental effect. It will steal your get-up-and-go. Bob Marley is reputed to have smoked an ounce of pot every day. I wouldn't recommend that, but I have enjoyed it once in a blue moon.

Similarly, I think popping pills every weekend is equally stupid and destructive, but I'm a realist and I live life to the fullest, and given my personality type, I was bound to experiment. My attitude to life is to have a crack, so when I was offered Ecstasy, I did some research and then I tried it. I had no problem making that decision. I've always had gut feelings on things and I usually follow them. Once I make a decision I never have any trouble getting on with it. I took Ecstasy in a controlled environment. I understood what it was, what it was going to do, and the downside or the risks associated with it.

Matthew Ridge: For a guy who comes across as a larrikin, he's actually very conservative. He doesn't take many risks. He'll ponder and ponder and ask people about things before making a decision. That's the way he's been brought up and it's an intelligent way to be, but he doesn't come across that way on TV. He thinks about how he's perceived. He's very measured.

It's not ideal to now have a drug conviction, far from it. It's a badge I'll wear for life and something my children (if I'm lucky enough to have them) will someday have thrown in their face in the playground. One of the biggest negatives is that I can't travel.

I can't go back to the United States for at least three years and that's sad because New York's where I got engaged. That was hard, meeting Agustina in New York with all of the drug stuff about to blow up on my return home, and going through with the proposal I'd been planning for weeks. (In the end I think I did a pretty good job of just getting it out of my mind and enjoying the moment.) And it will be hard to be restricted when it comes to travelling now.

As much as no one ever wants to have to learn about themselves under stressful circumstances, I've learnt a lot from my drug conviction.

Ric Salizzo: I think it will be an important part of Marc's life, a life-changing experience. He took stock of where he was at and re-evaluated things. I'm not talking about drugs. Not the drugs side of it, but where he was at. He saw that he lived in a small town and shit happened. His life is quite different now to the period when the surveillance was happening. Now he's married, he's left Charlie's. He's shown how he deals with a tough time and I think he's won a lot of respect.

Chris Ellis: We've encouraged him to stand tall and we've encouraged him to learn from it and to think more clearly and think things through more. It hasn't changed him in any context, but it has had an effect on him.

I learnt that I'm pretty straight up and down, and stay that way no matter what pressure is on, and that I keep things in perspective. I'm a strong believer in fate — everything happens for a reason and, for whatever reason, this happened. I know I'm not a shit or a drug felon or a creep, but this is part of who I am now and I can't do anything about that. I might even see it as a positive experience at the end of the day.

Moving On

Prior to the 'drugs scandal', a few months before the last election, I received a call at work from the politician Murray McCully. He asked if I had any interest in politics. It struck me as being completely out of left field — why on earth would the National Party suggest I run for Parliament? I had to meet him.

We met at the Northern Club, a club I belong to in Auckland, and had a chat. That led to an invitation to meet Don Brash, the leader of the National Party. I went to Don's house for a cup of tea with him and his wife Je Lan. He asked if I would consider going on the list as a National candidate in the upcoming election. I said if I were to do it I would prefer to stand in an electorate rather than walk straight into Parliament, and I suggested that the only electorate for me to stand in would be Mount Albert. Against Helen Clark. I'd be on a hiding to nothing, but for me trying to climb Mount Everest holds more appeal than walking up One Tree Hill.

Tempting though the thought of ruffling a few feathers in Parliament was, after due consideration I declined. Sure, I think politics could do with some big changes. Politicians seem devoid of personality and humour, and afraid to make mistakes (when they do, they find it even harder to tell the truth and say they cocked up). They have no human face. Why do they all wear suits and ties and speak in legalese (when most of New Zealand doesn't understand it)? Why do they read from autocues, rather than speaking from the heart?

The only character left in New Zealand politics is Winston Peters. I'm not sure he believes what he says all the time, but he's fun to watch and listen to. He has charisma, so if there's a debate on, you want him to be in it. The same can't be said for the other political leaders.

My view is that we need politicians that appeal to average New Zealanders, not ones who pretend to be like us. But I won't be one of them. You have to have a real passion for politics to be a politician, and be ready for it to take over your life. There are a lot of things I believe in strongly, but not enough to make a career of politics. It doesn't frustrate me enough to get involved in it. The scrutiny would be hard for me. I wouldn't like people looking for holes and trying to drag me down. It wasn't for me.

* * *

I got married early in 2006. Marriage is something I've always taken really seriously. Both Agustina's and my parents are still happily married and, knowing the support and love I've had from my folks, it was hard for me to imagine a scenario where I wouldn't eventually settle down.

For me, if you make that decision it's for life, for better or worse. You hang in there. It's taken me 34 years to get my head around that concept, and to meet the right person. In my late 20s I wasn't even thinking about marriage, but after meeting Agustina several years ago I started contemplating it.

Agustina's just cool. She is somebody that I know I'll be guessing about till the day I die. She's a bit mysterious and I like that, it suits my personality. I like the challenge. It's a great feeling to wake up in the morning, or go home at night, and see my best friend. And as long as we have a roof over our heads, close friends (and plenty of red meat to eat), we'll do OK. I am sure that this, not the artificial trimmings many of us aspire to, is the true key to success in life.

* * *

The big question now is: 'Where to next?' I really struggle with the answer to that one. I never could have predicted a decade ago that I'd be where I am today, so maybe I shouldn't try to guess where I might be 10 years from now.

I know I enjoy being creative and creating things others can enjoy — whether that's a product, a service or a concept — so future career plans will cater to that. I have experienced enough to know that I don't like to have my creativity stifled and I have promised myself that I will never let that happen. Anything that allows me to look out the window and dream will suit me.

I love travel and so does Agustina, so I figure that will be a priority in the future. I'm really looking forward to travelling more, maybe even spending quite a bit of each year overseas. I've never done an OE. When most of my mates took off to London I stayed here and made the most of the opportunities that came my way. I thought it would be silly not to stay and make hay while the sun shone, and because of the All Blacks and my TV work I got to see a huge part of the world.

I know I'm really lucky to have done that, but it was always on someone else's timetable. I got to scratch the surface of a lot of places, but I could never say, 'Hey, I wouldn't mind staying for another week'. I haven't ever entrenched myself in somewhere new, experienced the culture from the street. There's a part of me that would like to do that now, to go and get some experience living somewhere else. I'd love to go to Europe and park up in the south of France, learn the language, maybe open a café.

One thing I do know is that I must learn Spanish before we have children (it's Agustina's first language), otherwise I will really have the odds against me. The support my parents have shown me will give me a really cool blueprint for when Agustina and I have children and being a parent will be the biggest thing in my life. I think being a good parent will be how I judge just how successful I am.

So cheers for having sufficient interest in my story to read it. And here's hoping the next 10 years will be as eventful as the last.